BEEF *for* ALL SEASONS

ALSO BY FREDERICK J. SIMON

The Steaklover's Companion

PHOTOGRAPHS BY TIM TURNER

Presents: A Year of Beef Recipes

BEEF *for* ALL SEASONS

FREDERICK J. SIMON *and* JOHN HARRISSON

HarperCollins*Publishers*

HarperCollins books may be purchased for educational, business, or sales promotional use. For information please write: Special Markets Department, HarperCollins Publishers, Inc., 10 East 53rd Street, New York, NY 10022.

FIRST EDITION

Designed by Elina D. Nudelman

Library of Congress Cataloging-in-Publication Data

Simon, Frederick J., 1937–

    Beef for all seasons : a year of beef recipes / Frederick J. Simon and John Harrisson. — 1st ed.

      p.   cm.

    ISBN 0-06-019382-4

    I. Harrisson, John. II. Title.

TX749.5.B43S555   1999

641.6'62—dc21   99-15025

99 00 01 02 03 ❖/RRD 10 9 8 7 6 5 4 3 2 1

Dedicated to the culinary professionals of America,
the creative chefs and food preparers who enhance our lives
with memorable dining experiences

CONTENTS

ACKNOWLEDGMENTS

There is a love of food in my family. My late parents, Trudi and Lester Simon, cooked and served beef dishes with meat cuts provided by our family business, Omaha Steaks. My wife, Eve, is a natural cook. What she has learned over the years is now instinctive. When a recipe calls for many ingredients and processes, Eve does the cooking, always with great results.

I had the pleasure of working with the late James Beard, the dean of American cookery, for the last eleven years of his life. Initially, we met at a conference in Montreal, Canada, in 1973. He enjoyed our products, suggested new ones for our catalog business, and wrote many recipes for the Omaha Steaks recipe pamphlets. He was an extraordinary teacher; I listened and have never stopped learning. Because of Jim, dining became a most important and continuing life experience for me.

In our first book, *The Steaklover's Companion*, we used a regional approach to steak cooking and took a nine-chapter trip around the world. Essentially, the book was eighty steak recipes and their side dishes. This book, *Beef for All Seasons*, is a seasonal approach to beef, which includes recipes for various holidays and special occasions. We present beef recipes from around the world, and I am grateful to the many chefs who contributed their ideas and recipes.

Though I conceived the seasonal concept, my co-author, John Harrisson, developed most of the recipes. John was involved in all aspects of producing this book:

research, writing, recipe testing, photography, and organizing our team. His imagination and diligence and his knowledge of cookbook publishing was invaluable and kept me on track all through the process. John's own list of acknowledgments follows.

I am fortunate to have my son, Todd, as a business adviser. He was essential to me in the formation of our publishing goals.

Tim Turner, our photographer, created the succulent essence of thirty recipes through the camera's eye. Tim loves to cook and loved this project—and it shows. His photos go beyond beauty and accuracy. They guide our reader to a clear understanding of presentation and even a taste of the dish.

Susan Friedland, our editor at HarperCollins, deserves our thanks for accepting our second project, making appropriate suggestions about its scope, and helping us with her commonsense guidance. Her assistant, Ellen Morrissey, helped smooth the way at every turn, and we also owe her our thanks.

And finally, there are many associates and friends who helped and advised us throughout the process of producing this book. They include Jackie Thompson, Omaha Steaks staff home economist, for her careful proofreading; Bob Frank, wine expert, for his thoughtful wine selections; and Merle Ellis, "The Butcher," our friend and adviser. Many company employees were helpful with communications, administration, product preparation, and logistics and marketing: Deb Righter, Shari Gouldsmith, Dave Hershiser, Curt Todd, Bob Bezousek, Earlene Sterba, Neil Lucas, Jim Paschal, Lisa Nenneman, and Sharon Grunkin.

—F. S.

I blush at Fred's kind words, and rush to thank the many individuals without whom this project would have been a great deal harder. First, my wife, taste-tester extraordinaire, and an "editor's editor," Trez. She may not know too much about Hungarian soccer (see the recipe on page 21), but she knows a good cut of beef when she sees one. My late mother, Joan Harrisson, my first and best teacher, was a lover of cookbooks; she would have enjoyed this one.

My right arm (actually, my left arm—I'm a southpaw) during this project was Terry Finlayson. Her expertise, professionalism, and good taste made the process of recipe development and testing an enjoyable collaborative effort (I mention more about Terry on page 91). Terry was in turn aided and abetted by Carol Scudder, Linda Perme, and Sharon Lewis.

Kathy Long, instructor at the Santa Fe School of Cooking and food writer, also made much-appreciated contributions to this book.

I am indebted to the incredibly creative chefs who either contributed recipes to this book, or provided inspiration with their genius. I am proud to call many of them my good friends: Hubert Keller, Stephan Pyles, John Sedlar, Norman Van Aken, Alan Wong, Roy Yamaguchi, Mark Miller, Emeril Lagasse, Chris Schlesinger, and Lionel Havé.

Finally, my thanks to you, Fred, for your integrity, generosity, and above all, your friendship. It is always a pleasure working with you.

—J. H.

AMERICA LOVES BEEF

Foreword by Mark Miller

American culinary history is so closely linked with beef that, from the earliest days, one cannot think of one without the other. We have become a nation of beef eaters, and beef is the national meat of choice. The lore of cattle and the cowboy is part of our mythology to such an extent that the West and the cow are linked forever in our consciousness. Some would even say that symbols like McDonald's, barbecue, and fat juicy steaks represent the gospel of beef converting the rest of the world, so that eating beef is not just a food choice but a way of life.

There is no region of American cuisine or facet of American life that is not represented by beef in some form: the boiled dinners of New England; the pastrami sandwiches of New York City; the country-fried steaks with smothered gravy of the South; the grilled, extra-thick cut of Kansas City strip; Midwestern meat loaves; bowls of steaming, thick, all-beef chili with cornbread in Texas; the spaghetti and meatballs of San Francisco's North Beach; and the sizzling platters of beef fajitas with warm tortillas of Southern California and the Southwest.

American lifestyle is defined by beef: We have hot dogs at ball games, hamburgers on the Fourth of July, and roasted prime rib at Christmas. When we are old enough to go to school, Mom makes us bologna sandwiches, and a little later, our favorite food is hamburger. Kids just cannot get enough hamburger. Then we grow up into teenagers and as soon as we can drive we eat more hamburgers (and fries), hanging out at burger joints and diners after school, games, and dances. Once we graduate or receive our first big raise, we celebrate with a fancy steak dinner and an expensive bottle of wine. Later still, we celebrate important anniversaries with a succulent grilled filet mignon. Beef is always there in our important meals, the rituals that create meaning in our lives.

Beef has been around in my own culinary history throughout my cooking career. In my student days I experimented, cooking simple dishes with inexpensive cuts of beef; no, I did not buy hamburger all the time! I learned to identify the different cuts that needed to be slowly braised to make interesting, tender dishes, or that could be skillet-fried. One of my most memorable early achievements came after watching Julia Child make boeuf bourgignon on television. I browned the meat very carefully and poured in the best jug wine from the local Wine Barrel. I added herbs and vegetables and stewed it gingerly for hours. Then I packed it up and took it with me to Yosemite, where twelve of my closest friends and I devoured it by moonlight after a hard day's hiking. Instantly my status was elevated to that of culinary wizard, and best of all, I didn't have to clean up! (To me, that is one of the great joys of doing the cooking—you have all the fun and can delegate the work involved in cleaning up to others).

Later on, when I started working at Chez Panisse in Berkeley, we made some fantastic beef dishes. One of the most memorable was a simple one that the chef Jean Pierre Moulet loved to prepare—beef *en ficelle*, literally, beef on a string. The dish was simple, but to me it embodied the very essence of beef. You take a beef filet that has been dry-aged for two or three weeks, trim up the outside, and cut it across the grain into 12-ounce portions. Then you wrap the beef with butcher's twine, leaving a two-foot length of string, and drop the filet into a stockpot of simmering double-strength beef stock. You cook it until it is rose-colored and still juicy and then haul it up with the string. After cutting the string and unwrapping the beef, you serve it with buttery braised leeks, new potatoes, baby carrots, and whole-grain mustard, with good-quality crunchy sea salt to dip into. This will be a memorable meal, and the best boiled dinner you've ever tasted.

When I opened my own restaurant, Fourth Street Grill in Berkeley, we served the best hamburgers in the Bay Area, as chosen in a local readers' poll. We used freshly ground beef, minced serrano chiles, freshly chopped herbs, and freshly cracked pepper, and we took care to grill them to perfect doneness over mesquite coals. At my next Berkeley restaurant, Santa Fe Bar and Grill, we served one of the all-time great beef dishes: Paul Prudhomme's blackened Cajun grilled beef filet with a spicy beef sauce. The sauce was the key part of the recipe and took three days to make. It was made with blackened beef bones, tons of vegetables, and spices galore that we cooked for two days, strained, and cooked again. It was unbelievably intense and fulfilling.

At Coyote Café, which I opened in Santa Fe in 1987, one of our trademark dishes has become our famous Cowboy Steak—an aged, 22-ounce bone-in rib-eye served with red chile onion rings. Other favorites are beef tartare with chipotle chiles, and grilled beef filet wrapped with prosciutto and served with a black truffle hollandaise. Beef presents endless possibilities for the chef and home cook alike.

As this book so aptly proves, beef has been adopted as common culinary currency all over the world, and I have many wonderful memories of great beef dinners enjoyed around the globe. For example, and just to pick a few: The churasco grills of Brazil with long, flame-broiled skewers holding an array of cuts; the Argentine steak houses that are truly a hell for vegetarians (the only nonbeef offering seems to be the tomato salad). Here, the intense flavor of grass-fed cattle contrasts with the pronounced oregano tones of the picante chimichurri sauce. In Japan I have enjoyed rich beef sukiyaki simmered in a sauce started with a melting piece of beef suet and made with sake, sugar, and soy. The beef, dipped in a clinging egg yolk, was served with perfect rice. In Southeast Asia I remember a Thai beef salad consisting of thin slices of rare grilled beef served with a pungent sauce over rice noodles and accented with chiles, Thai basil, and lemongrass. The goulashes of Hungary, made with simmered onions and sweet red paprika, topped off with thick sour cream, are another of my fondest beef memories (the goulash recipe that follows in this book should evoke a similar response).

Just as we have exported the hamburger to the rest of the world, so Americans have embraced countless new ways of preparing and cooking beef. I think we got the better part of that culinary trade! Today's generation of kids is lucky: They are able to enjoy the best beef with the best flavors from all over the world, and this book will help bring some of those recipes into the home kitchen. Beef always fits the occasion and the mood, whatever the season. It is nothing if not versatile. Whether it's a steak sandwich, barbecued brisket, braised short ribs, or a more sophisticated grilled steak or pastry-covered beef en croute, beef satisfies.

If the lion is the king of the jungle, then beef is the king of the table! It fulfills the hunger of the soul and satiates the beast within, especially when you crave a dining experience that is timeless in flavor and value. Beef comforts us, and its complex yet simple quality invariably fits our mood. Nothing else seems to bring such apparent pleasure to dinner guests' faces. Best of all, anything that has been this popular for thousands of centuries can hardly be described as trendy. Truly, beef is a food for all occasions, and for all seasons.

INTRODUCTION

Well, the devil has obviously been slipping up on the job in recent years as the standard of the professional culinary arts—and that of cooking in the home—has been raised to ever new heights. The revolution in American food that began in the 1970s—brought about by greater health awareness, increased travel to other countries, and the emergence of many talented and charismatic young chefs (among other factors)—has changed the way we think about food. It has also changed the way we cook. Heaven still sends us good beef; not only that, but its quality has improved over the last few decades to meet the market demand for leaner, more healthful cuts.

Call us biased, but beef is surely the best-loved meat of choice not only in the United States, but in many other countrenses—like the hearty, rich flavor of beef. The sizzle and aroma of a beef roast; the sumptuous texture of filet mignon; the complex flavors and "mouth-feel" of a really superb casserole; the deliciously charred character of a juicy grilled steak all conspire to set the mouth watering and the taste buds tingling. Nowadays, as we face a new millennium, beef has recovered its popularity and steak houses are popping up everywhere. Not only has beef been bred leaner but savvy consumers now consume smaller portions of better-trimmed meat and they have come to value the significant nutritional value of beef. As the trend has been toward smaller, more affordable portions, people are seeking the best, so we encourage the purchase of prime or choice beef,

> Heaven sends us good meat, but the devil sends us cooks.
>
> —DAVID GARRICK, EIGHTEENTH-CENTURY ENGLISH ACTOR

which have a little more fat; both prime and choice are well marbled and therefore more juicy, tender, and flavorful. As people's diets have become more varied and beef is less of an everyday food, it has become more appreciated. This sensible approach, away from prodigious slabs of beef and toward thoughtful moderation, is welcomed.

Beef is a "centerpiece" ingredient that can be enjoyed year round, which is why we decided to write this book. Our first cookbook, *The Steak Lover's Companion*, featured—you guessed it—steaks, and a great many folk associate steaks with the summer grilling season. Others think of beef as rich and filling, and therefore something to be enjoyed mostly on cold winter evenings. The recipes in this book prove that there is far more to the summer season than steaks, and that seasonal ingredients can be used all year long to complement and highlight the many roles that beef can play on the plate. They show that beef is nothing if not versatile. The recipes here include soups, salads, appetizers, and main courses, either grilled, braised, seared, barbecued, sautéed, broiled, and roasted—there's never a dull moment when you put your mind to preparing beef. So this book has something for everyone, for any time of the year.

As with *The Steak Lover's Companion*, many of the recipes in this book were contributed—or inspired by—some of this country's leading chefs. Emeril Lagasse, John Sedlar, Hubert Keller, Norman Van Aken, Mark Miller, Alan Wong, Stephan Pyles, and Chris Schlesinger are among the stars represented here. Recipes by James Beard, the godfather of modern American cooking and a consultant to Omaha Steaks for many years, are also featured. Inspiration comes from unexpected places—from Dr. Johnson to LBJ to a Hungarian soccer star to Jimi Hendrix (to name a few). There are few parts of the world not represented in these pages, one way or

Beef is a "centerpiece" ingredient that can be enjoyed year round

another. From America's heartland and far-flung regions we make stops in England, Scotland, France, Italy, Germany, Hungary, Russia, the Middle East, China, India, Thailand, Japan, Hawaii, Mexico, the Caribbean, and South America—quite a journey! We put new spins on old classics and proudly present many new ideas.

Each recipe in this book features an accompaniment—often, a starch as well as a vegetable—and where appropriate, a sauce or side of some kind. While we think the combinations fit together well, you should feel free to "mix and match," to "chop and change," and to substitute your own favorite side dishes. Likewise, experiment with different cuts of beef to gain an appreciation of the qualities that each possesses, and to master the cooking techniques that best suit them. We hope these recipes add to your culinary repertoire and your enjoyment of our favorite meat.

Each recipe includes a sidebar that contains helpful cooking tips, information about ingredients or methods, or alternatives and substitutions, as well as suggested wines to accompany the meal. In most cases, we have recommended two or more wines; usually, one from the United States, and one or more from France, Italy, or elsewhere in Europe. A section that follows provides definitions of ingredients and equipment and a glossary of terms. A chapter of basic recipes and techniques is included after the main seasonal recipe chapters.

We suggest that you review each recipe carefully before embarking on its preparation, not only to make sure that you have all the ingredients but to arrive at a realistic estimate of how long the recipe will take. There are quick recipes here, and ones that take longer—some require marinating for several hours, for example.

BEEF: TECHNIQUES AND TIPS
As Recommended by Omaha Steaks

STORING AND HANDLING

Beef, like meat of all kinds, should be refrigerated as soon as possible after purchase and kept refrigerated. Cook beef as soon as possible after purchasing, or at least within a reasonable amount of time (preferably no more than 2 or 3 days). If using meat that has been frozen, or if you choose to buy beef that has been shipped with dry ice or a freezer pack, be sure to thaw in the refrigerator—this allows for juicier, more flavorful results. Never thaw meat at room temperature. Thawing vacuum-sealed beef in cold water will speed the process; using a microwave is the least recommended method. Cuts of beef that have been thawed in the refrigerator but either contain ice crystals or are still cold to the touch (at or below 40 degrees) and have been held in the refrigerator for only a day or two, can be refrozen. Seal the meat tightly in freezer bags with as little air inside as possible, and for best results, use within 3 months.

To ensure safe handling of meat, do not use the same cutting board or platter for raw meats and cooked meats. Thoroughly wash hands, utensils, cutting boards, and countertops that come into contact with raw food. Once cooked, do not let meats stand at room temperature, but refrigerate leftovers immediately.

COOKING BEEF

It is always preferable to cook beef from a thawed state. There are several common methods for cooking

> **The best test of doneness is to remove the beef and to cut into it with a sharp knife.**

meat: grilling, broiling, sautéing, roasting, and braising. In the case of the first two methods, it is important to preheat the grill or broiler; for sautéing, heat the pan until it is hot before adding the meat, so the juices are effectively sealed in. For roasting and braising, preheat the oven and begin cooking only when the oven reaches the temperature called for in the recipe.

When grilling, with either a gas or charcoal grill, using a lid will make it easier to regulate the temperature over which you are cooking. Note that keeping a lid on will speed up cooking time and reduce flare-ups. Make sure the charcoals are covered with a thin layer of gray ash and have a red glow before adding the beef. Broiling is a high heat method; the steaks should be at least 2 to 3 inches away, and up to 4 or 5 inches from the heat source. When broiling with an electric oven, leave the oven ajar. Use heavy pans or skillets when sautéing beef, so the heat is evenly distributed across the bottom of the pan and the meat cooks evenly. Roasting can be done either quickly, at high temperatures, or slowly, at lower temperatures. The meat should be placed in the center of the oven. Braising is a technique often used for tougher cuts of meat that require a long cooking time to become perfectly tender.

In timing beef as it cooks, remember that bone-in cuts will take longer than boneless ones. The cooking times given in the recipes are given as general guidelines rather than hard-and-fast rules, and there are many factors that can affect timing. When grilling, for example, the exact size and heat of the fire tends to vary, and factors such as weather (especially wind, humidity, and air temperature), the openness of air vents, the height of the grill rack, and placement of the meat on the grill can each affect exact cooking times. Likewise, gauging "medium-high heat" when sautéing on a gas stove is a rather imprecise and subjective measure, while it generally takes longer to adjust the heat using an electric stove. The exact thickness of meat will also affect recommended cooking times, so be flexible.

When grilling, keep the rack clean with a wire brush and wash the rack after each use. In most cases, lightly oiling the rack before grilling the steaks will prevent them from sticking, especially if they have been coated with a dry rub.

The best test of doneness is to remove the beef and to cut into it with a sharp knife. You may find it easier to use an instant-read meat thermometer, which can be inserted into the center of the cut. Bear in mind that internal temperature will rise 5 to 10 degrees after removing the meat from the heat. Therefore, at the time you stop the cooking process, the internal temperature should be 120 degrees for rare; 130 degrees for medium-rare; 140 degrees for medium; and 150 degrees for medium-well. Another means of testing beef—and especially steaks—for doneness is to touch it with your finger. Rare steak meat will feel soft and wobbly, while at medium, it will have a springy firmness. Well-done steak will feel very firm and unyielding.

In general, season steaks before you put them on the grill; some of the seasoning will burn off and some will marry with the outside of the meat, giving you just the flavor you're looking for. Thickness is important. Thicker steaks are more easily controlled regardless of the cooking method, so for best results, purchase steaks at least 1 to 1¼ inches thick—1½ inches is even better. Turn steaks as they cook just once; they should be turned when the meat juices begin to bubble up through the meat to the top of the steaks. The recipes in this book call for an even cooking time for each side, but some cooks prefer to cook the first side a little longer than the second, since the second side will be warming even while it is away from direct heat. For example, if the recipe calls for cooking a steak for 4 minutes per side, you might want to cook the first side for 5 minutes and the second for 3.

Use whichever method suits your personal preference, and test the steaks for doneness as they cook.

Be aware that beef will continue to cook a little even after you remove it from the heat source. For smaller cuts such as steaks, it is best to stop cooking at the point when they test slightly less done than desired.

Finally, a word about portion sizes: Most of the recipes in this book serve main course portions, and assume healthy appetites. While most meat portions fall within the 6 to 8 ounce range, others call for more—for example, 16-ounce bone-in Porterhouse steaks. By all means choose smaller cuts that fit within your budget and appetite, or if you are particularly concerned about your diet. Once again, use your judgment and adjust the recipes accordingly.

DEFINITIONS AND GLOSSARY OF TERMS

DEFINITIONS OF INGREDIENTS AND EQUIPMENT

All ingredients are medium size, unless stated otherwise.

Onions, garlic, carrots, and ginger are all peeled, unless stated otherwise.

Chiles and bell peppers are seeded, unless stated otherwise.

Herbs are fresh, unless stated otherwise; bay leaves are dried, and removed from a dish before it is served.

Butter is unsalted, unless stated otherwise

Eggs are extra-large, unless stated otherwise

Chicken stock is a good-quality, low-sodium canned variety; by all means make your own and use that.

"Light" soy sauce means that it is lower in sodium and therefore less salty than regular soy sauce.

Salt and pepper "to taste": start by seasoning in small increments, tasting as you go, until you reach the desired flavor. Remember, you can always add more at the table, so err on the side of caution.

Chipotle chiles en adobo are canned (chipotle chiles are also available dried, in which case they need rehydrating). "En adobo" refers to the spicy pickling liquid in which the chiles are packed. Chipotles are smoked jalapeños, and they have a hot, smoky flavor.

Garam masala is a ready-made spice blend that is popular in the cuisine of northern India. Typically, it contains toasted spices such as coriander, cumin, cinnamon, cloves, nutmeg, fennel, mace, and chile powder.

Toasted sesame oil is the dark brown, fragrant, and strongly flavored oil favored in Asian cooking. It is a different product than regular sesame oil, which is much lighter in color.

Zest of citrus fruit is the aromatic, outermost layer of the skin; that is, it excludes the bitter white pith. Citrus zest can be removed with a zester, vegetable peeler, or a sharp knife.

All bowls and pans used are nonreactive (ceramic, glass, or stainless steel). Avoid aluminum cookware.

GLOSSARY OF TERMS

Deglaze: adding a liquid such as water, wine, or stock to a cooking pan and stirring to dislodge food particles that are stuck to the pan.

Dice: cutting ingredients into neat ½-inch-cube shapes (the shape of dice). "Finely diced" or "cut into small dice" refers to ¼-inch cubes, while "cut into large dice" refers to ¾-inch cubes. Larger cuts are considered "chopped"; smaller ones are referred to as "minced."

Julienne: cutting ingredients (usually vegetables) into sticks, about ⅛ inch wide and 1 or 2 inches long.

Mince: cutting food very finely and neatly. Minced ingredients are less coarsely cut than diced or chopped ones.

Reduce: Cooking a liquid rapidly to decrease its volume by evaporation and to thicken it and concentrate its flavors.

Sear: Browning meat or other food quickly over high heat, usually as a prelude to further cooking. Searing meat seals in its natural juices.

Sweat: Cooking an ingredient (usually vegetables) in a small amount of oil over low heat to soften and release moisture, and to avoid coloration.

BEEF *for* ALL SEASONS

I. RECIPES FOR SPRING

RECIPES FOR SPECIAL OCCASIONS

**Curried Beef Samosas with Roasted
Eggplant–Mint Raita, page 14**

EMERIL'S SKILLET STEAK WITH TASSO MAQUE CHOUX AND FRIED CHANTERELLES

Serves 4

Emeril Lagasse is by now one of America's best-known and best-loved chefs, thanks to his personable style on such TV shows as *Good Morning America* and *The Essence of Emeril*, broadcast by the Food Network. He has also become a household name through his cookbooks, including *Emeril's New New Orleans Cooking*, and *Louisiana Real and Rustic*. About this recipe, Emeril says, "This dish is a union of the best things Louisiana has to offer, including spicy tasso, Creole seasoning, locally grown chanterelles, and maque choux, as well as the Southern comfort of a fried steak. Maque Choux—pronounced 'mock shoo'—a fantastic accompaniment with skillet steak, is a spicy Cajun dish of corn and seasonings, and every Cajun family has its own variation."

· ·

To prepare the maque choux, heat the olive oil in a large skillet over high heat. When the oil is hot, add the tasso and sauté for 30 seconds. Add the corn and cook for 1 minute longer, shaking and flipping the pan frequently. Add the onion and sauté for 30 seconds more. Add the garlic, salt, and pepper, and cook for 1 minute. Stir in the cream, bell pepper, and scallions, and simmer until heated through, about 2 minutes. Remove from the heat and set aside.

Combine all the Creole seasoning ingredients in a mixing bowl and reserve 5 teaspoons (store the remainder in an airtight jar or container for further use).

Trim the layer of fat from 1 edge of each strip steak,

FOR THE TASSO MAQUE CHOUX:

2 tablespoons olive oil
⅓ cup diced tasso or
   spiced ham
1½ cups fresh corn
   kernels (from 2 ears
   corn)
⅓ cup chopped onion
1 tablespoon minced
   garlic
1 teaspoon salt
Pinch of freshly ground
   black pepper
1 cup heavy cream
⅓ cup minced red bell
   pepper
⅓ cup chopped scallions

For Emeril's Creole Seasoning:

2½ tablespoons mild
   paprika
2 tablespoons salt
1 tablespoon freshly
   ground black pepper
2 tablespoons garlic
   powder
1 tablespoon onion
   powder
1 tablespoon cayenne
1 tablespoon dried
   oregano
1 tablespoon dried
   thyme

For the Steaks:

4 strip sirloin steaks,
   7 to 8 ounces each, or
   boneless rib-eye steaks
1 tablespoon olive oil

For the Mushrooms:

3 cups plus 1 tablespoon
   vegetable oil
½ cup all-purpose flour
16 chanterelle
   mushrooms, or 12
   small cultivated
   mushrooms, cut in
   half, cleaned
Salt to taste

4 sprigs thyme, for
   garnish

leaving the thicker piece of fat attached to help the meat keep its shape. (Omit this step if using rib-eye steak.) Sprinkle each steak with ½ teaspoon of the seasoning and pat in well with the palm of your hand or the side of a heavy knife. Heat the olive oil in a large cast-iron skillet set over high heat. When the oil is smoking, add the steaks and sear for 2 to 2½ minutes per side for rare, 3 minutes per side for medium-rare, or to desired doneness. (Rib-eye steaks will take 30 seconds to 1 minute longer on each side.) Remove from the heat.

While the steaks are cooking, prepare the mushrooms. Heat 3 cups of the vegetable oil in a saucepan set over high heat. Combine the flour with the remaining 3 teaspoons of the reserved Creole seasoning in a bowl. Place the remaining 1 tablespoon of vegetable oil in a saucer, dip the chanterelles in the oil, and then dredge in the seasoned flour, shaking off any excess. When the oil in the pan is smoking hot, add the chanterelles and fry until golden brown, about 1 to 2 minutes. Drain on paper towels and sprinkle with salt to taste.

To serve, place 1 cup of the maque choux on each serving plate. Place a steak on top of the maque choux and arrange the mushrooms on top. Garnish each steak with a sprig of thyme.

Wine Suggestion: *West Coast Pinot Noir or Bordeaux (less than 10 years old).*

This is a filling dish as it is, but if you wish, serve with mashed potatoes. The recipe is from *Emeril's New New Orleans Cooking* (1993), published by William Morrow and Company, and used here by permission.

BEEF EN DAUBE WITH POLENTA, GLAZED SHALLOTS, AND CABERNET SAUCE

Serves 4

Here's a recipe that's perfect for those chilly early spring evenings, and it's also ideal for late fall or winter. Beef en daube is a classic French stew named for the covered casserole, the *daubière*, in which it is prepared. Although the dish varies from region to region, it is usually made with meat and vegetables and slowly braised in a rich red wine and beef broth. Results are even better when braised a day in advance and the finished daube is refrigerated overnight, allowing the flavors to marry. Alternative side dishes for the polenta are rice, egg noodles, mashed potatoes, or kasha.

....

Combine the beef, onions, carrots, garlic, orange zest, cloves, allspice, bay leaf, and red wine in a large nonreactive mixing bowl. Marinate overnight in the refrigerator. Drain the beef, reserving the wine, orange zest, and bay leaf; remove the cloves and discard. Separate the beef from the vegetables. Pat the beef dry with paper towels.

Sauté the bacon in a large Dutch oven or ovenproof casserole over medium heat for 3 minutes, or until all the fat is released. Remove the bacon, chop, and set aside. Add the beef to the Dutch oven and cook for 8 to 10 minutes, stirring occasionally, until browned on all sides (to avoid crowding the pan, you may need to do this in 2 or 3 batches). Remove with a slotted spoon and set aside. Add the onions, carrots, and garlic to the Dutch oven and sauté for 5 or 6 minutes, until light

FOR THE DAUBE:

2 pounds lean chuck
   steak, cut into 1½-inch
   cubes
2 onions, diced
3 carrots, diced
3 garlic cloves, thinly
   sliced
1 (2-inch) piece of orange
   zest
4 cloves
Pinch of ground allspice
1 bay leaf
2 cups Cabernet wine
   (see Wine Suggestion,
   page 9)
6 slices bacon
1 tablespoon sugar
2 cups Beef Stock (page
   200)
Salt and coarsely ground
   black pepper to taste

For the Glazed Shallots:

1 tablespoon extra-virgin olive oil
12 large shallots, peeled
½ teaspoon sugar
¼ teaspoon salt
2 tablespoons balsamic vinegar

For the Polenta:

4 cups chicken stock
1 cup polenta or coarse cornmeal
3 tablespoons freshly grated Parmesan cheese
2 tablespoons butter
2 tablespoons sour cream (optional)
1 teaspoon freshly ground black pepper
Salt to taste

1 tablespoon chopped parsley

golden brown (if necessary, add a little olive oil to prevent the vegetables from sticking). Add the sugar and toss lightly to coat the vegetables. Caramelize the vegetables over medium heat for 4 to 5 minutes while stirring.

Preheat the oven to 350 degrees. Add the beef stock and the reserved red wine to the vegetables, add the reserved orange zest and bay leaf, and scrape the bottom of the pan with a spatula or spoon to incorporate any drippings. Return the beef and bacon to the pan and season with salt and pepper to taste. Bring the daube to a simmer on top of the stove, cover, and set in the middle of the oven. Cook for 2 to 2½ hours, until the beef is tender but not falling apart.

While the daube is cooking, prepare the glazed shallots. Heat the olive oil in a saucepan (preferably nonstick) and add the whole shallots. Cover the pan and sauté over low heat, until softened, about 15 to 20 minutes, turning occasionally. Remove the lid, add the sugar and salt, and toss lightly to coat the shallots. Caramelize the shallots over medium heat for 1 or 2 minutes while stirring. Turn down the heat, add the balsamic vinegar, and continue to cook while stirring until the vinegar evaporates. Keep warm, or reheat prior to serving.

About 30 minutes before serving, prepare the polenta. In a large heavy saucepan, bring the stock to a boil over high heat. Add the polenta in a steady but slow stream while whisking. Turn down the heat to low and continue to whisk for 25 minutes or until the polenta thickens (thin with a little more stock or water if necessary). Stir in the cheese, butter, sour cream, and pepper, and season with salt. Keep warm.

Remove the daube from the oven and adjust the seasonings. Remove and discard the orange zest and bay leaf. Spoon the polenta into warm shallow serving bowls and serve the daube next to the polenta. Place 3 glazed shallots on top of the daube on each plate and garnish with the chopped parsley.

Precut and trimmed carrots now available on the market are attractive in this dish. Use about 8 ounces (half of a bag) rather than 3 whole carrots. Another helpful tip: The beef can be loosely tied in cheesecloth before marinating to make it easier to separate from the vegetables at cooking time. If the broth is not as thick as you would like at the end of the cooking process, remove the meat and vegetables with a slotted spoon, place the Dutch oven on top of the stove, and reduce over medium heat until the desired consistency is reached.

DEVILED SHORT RIBS WITH DRUNKEN BEANS

Serves 4

For the Marinade:

¾ cup olive oil

4 tablespoons freshly
squeezed lime juice

¼ cup Dijon mustard

1½ tablespoons hot pure
red chile powder

1½ tablespoons brown
sugar

1 onion, finely diced

3 garlic cloves, minced

2 teaspoons salt

1 teaspoon ground black
pepper

¾ teaspoon ground
cumin

¾ teaspoon ground
allspice

For the Beef

4 pounds bone-in beef
short ribs, trimmed
and cut into 2-inch
lengths

Short ribs, cut into 2-inch lengths, are a mouthwatering delicacy when cooked perfectly. If you enjoy spicy, complex, rich flavors, then this is the dish for you!

Mix all the marinade ingredients together in a mixing bowl, stirring until the sugar dissolves. Add the ribs and marinate for 6 to 8 hours, or at least 3 hours, turning occasionally.

Rinse the drained beans under cold running water and transfer to a saucepan, covering with 2 to 3 inches of water. Bring to a boil, reduce the heat to a simmer, and cook for 1½ to 2 hours, or until only just tender. Add more water as necessary to keep the beans covered while cooking. Drain and reserve the beans. Heat the olive oil in a large sauté pan and cook the onion, garlic, and chiles for 5 minutes. Add the beans, tomatoes, beer, and salt, stir well, and bring to a boil. Reduce heat to a simmer and cook for about 15 minutes, until just a little liquid remains.

While the beans are cooking, preheat the oven to 450 degrees. Remove the ribs from the marinade, reserving the marinade, and place the ribs on a rack in a roasting pan lined with foil. Roast for 25 minutes, and then reduce the oven temperature to 350 degrees. Transfer the ribs to a clean roasting pan and add the marinade. Cover and cook for 1 hour longer, or until completely tender. Remove the ribs and keep warm. Scoop off the fat from the surface of the roasting pan and add the stock (mix the cornstarch or flour with 2 tablespoons of the stock in a cup first if you wish the sauce to have a thicker consistency).

Serve the short ribs with the sauce and beans. Garnish the beans with cilantro.

WINE SUGGESTION: *A zesty Pinot Noir from the West Coast or a regional Burgundy to complement the richness of this dish.*

> If your guests are hungry, serve with sweet Cinnamon-Cactus Rice (page 87). Finish the ribs on the grill for 5 to 10 minutes to give them an irresistible smoky flavor.

FOR THE BEANS:

1 cup dried pinto beans (8 ounces), soaked overnight and drained
1 tablespoon olive oil
½ onion, finely diced
2 garlic cloves, minced
2 jalapeño chiles, seeded and minced
4 Roma tomatoes (about 8 ounces), diced
½ bottle dark beer (such as Negro Modelo)
¼ teaspoon salt

1 cup warm Beef Stock (page 200)
½ tablespoon cornstarch or flour (optional)

4 teaspoons minced cilantro leaves, for garnish

GARLIC-STUFFED RIB-EYE STEAKS WITH CREAMY GARLIC CHARD

Serves 4

FOR THE STEAKS:

4 rib-eye steaks, 8 ounces each and about 1 inch thick

8 garlic cloves, cut into thick slivers

Salt and freshly ground black pepper to taste

2 tablespoons olive oil

As the title suggests, you've got to like garlic to fully enjoy this dish. It'll keep vampires away, that's for sure! If you prefer the garlic flavor a bit more mellow, you can roast the garlic cloves first; cook in the oven at 350 degrees for 10 minutes or dry-sauté in a heavy pan for about 5 minutes. For chile lovers, you might want to add some pep to the steaks by also adding some serrano or jalapeño slivers.

Stab the steaks on both sides with a sharp knife to make incisions and place the garlic slivers in the slits. Season the steaks with salt and pepper. Heat half of the oil in a heavy skillet or sauté pan and sauté 2 of the steaks over medium-high heat for about 3 minutes on each side for medium-rare, about 4 minutes for medium, or to desired doneness. Keep warm. Repeat for the remaining steaks.

To prepare the chard, heat 2 tablespoons of the butter in a sauté pan, add the chard, and cook over medium-high heat for 2 minutes, tossing frequently until wilted. Meanwhile, in a separate sauté pan, heat the remaining 1 tablespoon of butter. Add the garlic and onion and sauté for 5 minutes over medium-high heat until soft and translucent. Add the cream and bring to a boil. Add the chard and cook for 1 minute. Season with the nutmeg, salt, and pepper, and serve with the steaks.

WINE SUGGESTION: *A West Coast Pinot Noir or French Rhône wine will be powerful enough to match the assertive flavors of this dish.*

For a less creamy green vegetable dish, use the spinach recipe on page 40. If you wish, serve with roasted potatoes or one of the many potato recipes in this book.

FOR THE CREAMY GARLIC CHARD:

3 tablespoons butter

1 pound red chard, stems removed and cut in half crosswise

2 garlic cloves, minced

1 cup finely sliced onion

¼ cup heavy cream

⅛ teaspoon nutmeg, or to taste

Salt and freshly ground black pepper to taste

CURRIED BEEF SAMOSAS WITH ROASTED EGGPLANT–MINT RAITA

Yields 8 appetizers (about 24 samosas)

For the Samosas:

1 russet potato, about 8 ounces, peeled

1 tablespoon vegetable oil

½ onion, chopped

1 Granny Smith apple, peeled, cored, and chopped

2 tablespoons curry powder

¼ teaspoon cayenne, or to taste

1 (2-inch) length of cinnamon stick

¼ cup raisins

1 pound lean high-quality ground beef

1 can (14 ounces) crushed tomatoes, drained

1 cup frozen peas, rinsed under hot water

Salt and freshly ground black pepper to taste

Samosas make excellent appetizers or snacks, and fabulous hors d'oeuvres for parties or buffets. These triangular meat- or vegetable-filled pastries are commonly sold by vendors on street corners throughout India, although the fillings vary greatly. Here we combine ground beef, potatoes, and peas, seasoned with a sweet and savory curry. If you prefer a more highly seasoned curry, increase the amount of cayenne or sauté 1 or 2 minced red jalapeños or serranos with the onion. In India, the dough is made with flour and ghee (a type of clarified butter); however, egg roll wrappers (also labeled as spring roll wrappers) are an easy alternative. Raita (pronounced "right-ah") is a cooling yet flavorful accompaniment to curry dishes.

....

Preheat the oven to 350 degrees.

To prepare the samosas, boil the potato in a small saucepan of salted boiling water for 20 minutes, or until tender. When cool enough to handle, chop and set aside. Heat the vegetable oil in a large skillet, add the onion, and sauté over medium heat about 5 minutes, or until lightly golden. Add the apple and sauté for 2 to 3 minutes longer. Add the curry powder, cayenne, cinnamon stick, and raisins, and sauté for 3 to 4 minutes longer, stirring occasionally. Add the beef, and cook about 5 minutes or until just browned, using a kitchen fork to break up any lumps. Remove from the heat, drain off any fat, add the potato, tomatoes, and peas, and season with salt and pepper. Refrigerate for 2 to 3 hours. Meanwhile, prepare the raita.

1 eggplant, about 1
   pound
1½ cups whole-milk
   yogurt
2 tablespoons finely
   chopped mint
1 jalapeño chile, seeded
   and diced (optional)
Salt to taste
1 teaspoon freshly
   squeezed lemon juice,
   or to taste

12 large egg roll
   wrappers (6½ inches
   square)
2 teaspoons cornstarch
¼ cup water
3 cups vegetable oil, for
   frying
½ cup prepared mango
   chutney (optional)

Cut the eggplant in half lengthwise and lightly oil the cut side. Place cut side down on a baking sheet and roast in the oven until tender, 45 minutes to 1 hour. Remove from the oven. When cool enough to handle, remove the pulp, chop the flesh, and let cool completely. Transfer to a food processor or blender and puree with the yogurt, mint, and chile until relatively smooth but still a little chunky. Season with salt and lemon juice.

To finish the samosas, cut each egg roll wrapper in half lengthwise and lay it out on a work surface. Place a heaping teaspoon of the curried beef mixture at the corner of one end. Fold over the corner to form a triangle. Continue to fold like a flag, maintaining the triangular shape, until the whole strip is used. Mix the cornstarch and water in a cup and seal the edges of the samosas with the mixture.

Heat the vegetable oil in a heavy skillet over medium-high heat. When the oil is hot, add 5 or 6 of the samosas and cook, turning once, until both sides are golden brown, 3 to 4 minutes. Remove with a slotted spoon and drain on paper towels. Repeat for the remaining samosas, cooking them in small batches so they do not crowd the pan or lower the temperature of the oil. Keep the samosas in a warm oven until ready to serve. Serve the samosas with the raita and mango chutney.

WINE SUGGESTION: *A Beaujolais or a light-bodied West Coast Pinot Noir will provide the fruit and acidity that best matches this dish.*

The samosas may be prepared a day in advance but should be fried just before serving. If you don't need the whole batch, save some to fry the next day for snacks. Uncooked samosas can be frozen for a few weeks. Separate them with parchment or waxed paper and once thawed, be sure to dry them before frying. Leftover filling can be served over basmati rice, or stuffed in pita bread; see the Masala Sloppy Joes recipe on page 27 for an alternative samosa filling.

PINK PEPPERCORN STEAKS WITH BEURRE ROUGE AND SHOESTRING POTATOES

Serves 4

Pink peppercorns are aromatic, pungently flavorful, and unrelated to other types of peppercorns. In fact, they are not derived from the pepper plant at all. They are the dried berries of a type of rose grown only in Madagascar. Like black peppercorns, pink peppercorns accentuate the natural flavors of the beef, as does the beurre rouge, a red-hued variation of the classic French butter sauce beurre blanc. If you wish, serve this bistro-style dish with a crisp green salad and crusty French bread.

....

Soak the julienned potatoes in a bowl of cold water for about 30 minutes. Heat the oil in a deep-fryer or large saucepan to 375 degrees. Rinse the potatoes thoroughly, drain, and pat dry. Add the potatoes (in batches) to the hot oil and fry for about 2 or 3 minutes or until golden brown. (Keep the temperature of the oil constant during frying and between batches. If the oil becomes too hot, the fries will brown too quickly and will not stay crisp once removed from the fryer.) Remove with a slotted spoon, drain on paper towels, and season with salt. To keep warm, if necessary, place in an oven set on low heat. Do not cover, or the fries will become soggy.

Rub each steak with salt and about ½ tablespoon of the crushed pink peppercorns. Heat the olive oil in a large skillet and sear the steaks over medium-high heat until browned on both sides (about 1 minute per side). Turn the heat down to medium and continue to sauté

For the Shoestring Potatoes:

2 or 3 Idaho potatoes, about 8 ounces each, peeled and cut into ⅛-inch-thick to ¼-inch-thick julienne (preferably with a mandoline)

Peanut oil, for deep-frying

Salt

For the Steaks:

4 filet mignons, about 8 ounces each and 1¼ inches thick

Salt to taste

6 tablespoons pink peppercorns, crushed

1 tablespoon olive oil

the steaks for about 3 to 4 minutes on each side for medium-rare, 4 to 5 minutes for medium, or to the desired doneness.

To prepare the sauce, combine the red wine, red wine vinegar, and shallots in a saucepan and bring to a boil over medium-high heat. Reduce to about 2 tablespoons (this will take 10 to 15 minutes) and add the heavy cream. Turn the heat down to low and gradually add the butter, stirring slowly until it is all incorporated. Be careful not to let the mixture boil, or it will separate. Remove from the heat and strain if desired. Season with salt and the remaining ¼ cup of crushed pink peppercorns. Transfer to a double boiler or thermos flask to keep warm if not using immediately.

Arrange the steaks in the center of warm serving plates and garnish with the parsley. If you wish, pour any steak juices over the steaks. Ladle the sauce over the steaks and around the plate. Top with a heaping portion of fries.

WINE SUGGESTION: *A California Cabernet/Merlot blend or St. Émilion from Bordeaux.*

FOR THE BEURRE ROUGE:

½ cup red wine

¼ cup red wine vinegar

1 tablespoon minced shallots

1 tablespoon heavy cream

½ cup (4 ounces) butter, cut into cubes

¼ teaspoon salt

¼ cup crushed pink peppercorns (remaining from steak rub)

4 sprigs Italian flat-leaf parsley, for garnish

Although heavy cream is not an ingredient in the classic beurre blanc, chefs often use it to stabilize the sauce and prevent it from breaking up. Still, even with the heavy cream, this sauce will not hold for more than about 30 minutes. If you do not plan to serve the sauce immediately, you may wish to omit the heavy cream; otherwise, we strongly recommend it. The sauce is usually strained before serving, but we prefer to leave in the shallots and peppercorns for texture. The sauce reduction can be made in advance and finished with the butter after the steaks are cooked.

HAWAIIAN-STYLE SWEET-AND-SOUR BEEF RIBS WITH BAKED POTATOES

Serves 4

We swear, as soon as the sap begins to rise in spring and the air begins to warm up just a bit, the male genes kick in and out comes the barbecue grill. Well, for just that time, this is the perfect recipe! You get a bonus here because the sauce is not only sweet and sour, but a little hot, too—a tantalizing triple whammy. If you prefer, you may substitute such cuts of meat as flank steak or skirt steak, or even sirloin; the better the cut of beef, the less time needed to marinate. Serve with a green salad or steamed green beans, if you wish.

....

Place all the marinade ingredients in a mixing bowl, whisk together, and add the beef. Let marinate 6 to 8 hours, or at least 3 to 4 hours, stirring occasionally.

Preheat the oven to 400 degrees. Wash and dry the potatoes, pierce all over with a fork to prevent splitting, and rub with the oil. Place directly on a rack in the oven and bake for about 1 hour, or until tender when gently pierced with a fork. Remove from the oven and split open. Score the surface of the flesh with a knife, spread with the sour cream, and sprinkle with the chives.

While the potatoes are baking, prepare the grill (alternatively the beef can be broiled) and the sauce.

For the sauce, place the vinegar, mirin, soy sauce, peanut oil, ketchup, orange juice, and hot sauce in a saucepan and gently heat for 5 minutes over medium-low heat until warm. Mix together the cornstarch and water in a cup and add to the saucepan. Stir to combine

For the Marinade:
¼ cup toasted sesame oil
¼ cup peanut or olive oil
½ cup soy sauce
½ cup rice wine vinegar
½ cup sherry
¼ cup mirin
1 teaspoon minced garlic
1 teaspoon minced ginger

For the Beef:
2 pounds boneless beef short ribs, trimmed and cut into slices 4 to 5 inches long and ¼ inch thick

For the Potatoes:
4 baking potatoes, 8 to 10 ounces each
½ tablespoon olive oil
½ cup sour cream
4 teaspoons sliced chives

¼ cup rice wine vinegar

¼ cup mirin

1 tablespoon soy sauce

1 tablespoon peanut oil

2 tablespoons tomato
  ketchup

3 tablespoons freshly
  squeezed orange juice

½ tablespoon hot sauce
  (preferably with garlic,
  such as Sambal Oelek)

2 teaspoons cornstarch

¼ cup water

4 canned pineapple
  rings, finely diced

thoroughly, and add the pineapple. Keep warm.

Remove the beef from the marinade, letting any excess liquid drain off. Grill over medium heat for 5 to 6 minutes per side, or to the desired doneness. Transfer to serving plates, spoon the sauce over the beef, and serve with the baked potatoes.

WINE SUGGESTION: *A Japanese plum wine or a Barbera from California or Italy would provide the sweetness to complement the sweet-sour character of the food.*

The mirin used in the sauce is a flavorful Japanese rice wine seasoning. Its sweetness, together with the ketchup, means you don't need to add additional sugar.

BEEF GOULASH FERENC PUSKÁS–STYLE
Serves 6

The world owes Hungary for many things, one of which is goulash (or more properly, *gulyás*). Another is Ferenc Puskás, one of the greatest soccer players of all time. Puskás reached the zenith of his career in the 1950s, when the Hungarian national team was busy trouncing all comers. We feel certain Ferenc would approve of this dish, which reflects his game—robust and skillful. The addition of sun-dried tomatoes gives the goulash an intense and flavorful twist. The sour cream or yogurt, which cuts the richness of the dish, may be added to the whole dish before serving or by each guest at the table.

....

On a plate, mix the flour, salt, pepper, and cayenne. Dredge the beef in the flour mixture and set aside. Heat 2 tablespoons of the oil in a large nonstick sauté pan and sauté the garlic for 1 minute over medium-high heat. Add half of the dredged beef and sear over high heat for 5 minutes, or until browned on all sides. Remove from the pan and set aside. Add another 1 tablespoon of olive oil to the pan and sear the remaining beef. Set aside with the first batch.

Place the sun-dried tomatoes in a small bowl, add the water, and rehydrate for 10 minutes. When soft, remove from the water (reserving the water) and finely dice.

Heat the remaining 2 tablespoons of oil in a large saucepan and add the onions, shallots, and bell peppers. Sauté for 5 minutes over medium-high heat. Add the meat, tomatoes, paprika, red wine, beef stock, red wine

½ cup all-purpose flour
Salt and freshly ground black pepper to taste
Cayenne to taste
2 pounds beef tenderloin tips, choice grade, cut into ½-inch dice
5 tablespoons olive oil
2 garlic cloves, minced
2 ounces (1 cup) dried sun-dried tomatoes
1½ cups hot water
2 sweet onions, about 1 pound, diced
3 large shallots, about 6 ounces, diced
1 green bell pepper, seeded and diced
1 red bell pepper, seeded and diced
1 can (14 ounces) crushed tomatoes, with liquid
2 tablespoons mild paprika
¼ cup red wine (such as Italian Bardolino

2 cups Beef Stock (page
    200)
1 tablespoon red wine
    vinegar
2 bay leaves
1 teaspoon minced
    mixed herbs (such as
    parsley, chervil, and
    thyme)
¼ teaspoon ground
    cumin (optional)
1 cup sour cream or
    nonfat plain yogurt
1 pound wide egg
    noodles

2 teaspoons minced
    parsley, for garnish

The dish is best enjoyed with good crusty bread and hearty red wine (preferably the same used in the recipe). If you anticipate less robust appetites, omit the noodles and serve with bread or a little rice. Searing the beef in 2 batches gives the beef space to sear and prevents it from sticking together. For a spicier goulash, use a paprika with medium heat. Try to buy paprika in clear packages so you can see it; you know it's fresh if it's a vibrant brick red in color. Otherwise, buy it (and other dried herbs and spices) at a store where turnover is high.

vinegar, bay leaves, mixed herbs, cumin, sun-dried tomatoes, and reserved soaking water. Bring to a simmer, cover the pan, and simmer over low to medium-low heat for 1 to 1½ hours, or until the beef is perfectly tender, stirring occasionally. Add the sour cream and cook for 2 or 3 minutes, stirring to completely incorporate.

Meanwhile, prepare the egg noodles according to the instructions on the package (typically 10 to 12 minutes in boiling salted water). Drain. Discard the bay leaves from the goulash before serving. Serve the goulash on top of the noodles on serving plates. Garnish each serving with the parsley.

WINE SUGGESTION: *An Italian Bardolino or Egri Bikavér (Bull's Blood) from Hungary.*

STUFFED BEEF TOURNEDOS WITH FETTUCINE, SUN-DRIED TOMATOES, AND ZUCCHINI

Serves 4

This dish, redolent of the Mediterranean, is perfect for those late spring days when the heady days of summer and its bountiful harvest are just around the corner.

....

To prepare the tournedos, combine the tomatoes, olives, garlic, and thyme in a small bowl. Slice the tenderloin into 8 equal portions (about 3 ounces each); cut portions from the tapered end longer and flatten each steak so that the tournedos are approximately the same size. Cut a pocket in the side of each tournedo and fill with about 2 tablespoons of the sun-dried tomato–olive mixture. Season the steaks with pepper and set aside.

Cook the fettuccine *al dente*, according to the package directions. Drain, rinse, and set aside. Heat the olive oil in a large saucepan and sauté the onion over medium heat until translucent, about 5 minutes. Add the garlic and zucchini and sauté for 2 minutes longer. Add the tomatoes, sun-dried tomatoes, and thyme, and cook over medium heat for 3 to 4 minutes or until the mixture is relatively dry but still a little moist. Add the cooked fettuccine to the pan, stir in the heavy cream, and cook over low heat until the fettuccine is warm and the cream sauce thickens a bit. Season with the red pepper flakes, salt, and pepper.

To finish the steaks, heat the 1 tablespoon of olive oil in a large skillet and sauté the tournedos over medium-high heat for about 2 minutes per side for medium-rare,

FOR THE TOURNEDOS:

6 sun-dried tomatoes (packed in oil), minced

½ cup black olives (preferably Gaeta or Niçoise), pitted and minced (about ¼ cup)

2 tablespoons minced garlic

4 teaspoons minced thyme

1½ pounds center-cut beef tenderloin, prime or choice grade

1 teaspoon freshly ground black pepper

Fettuccine, Sun-dried Tomatoes, and Zucchini:

8 ounces dried fettuccine

1 tablespoon olive oil

1 onion, sliced

1 garlic clove, minced

1 zucchini, sliced

5 Roma tomatoes, blanched (page 207), peeled, seeded, and diced

6 sun-dried tomatoes (packed in oil), thinly sliced

½ teaspoon chopped thyme

¼ to ½ cup heavy cream

¼ teaspoon dried red pepper flakes

Salt and freshly ground black pepper to taste

1 tablespoon olive oil

¼ cup toasted pine nuts (page 210)

about 2½ minutes per side for medium, or to the desired doneness. Serve 2 tournedos per person, with the fettuccine on the side. Garnish the fettuccine with toasted pine nuts before serving.

Wine Suggestion: *Spanish Rioja or Penedès, or a California Petite Syrah.*

Like tournedos, filet mignon is also cut from the tenderloin; the only difference is that filets are thicker. If you wish, therefore, you can make tournedos by cutting plump (2-inch-thick) filet mignons in half crosswise.

JAMES BEARD'S "SONS OF REST" BEEFSTEAKS WITH SOUR CREAM–GRATIN POTATOES

Serves 4

We have adapted this recipe by an old friend of Omaha Steaks and a longtime consultant, the late James Beard. Jim, as he was known to his friends, was the dean, or godfather, of modern American cooking, influencing countless chefs with his enthusiastic endorsement and encouragement of home-grown cuisine and talent. He claimed that this old steak recipe was of anonymous origin, "although the Sons of Rest evidently relished good food!"

•••

Preheat the oven to 375 degrees.

Place the potatoes in a saucepan of lightly salted water and bring to a boil. Cook the potatoes at a low boil until just tender, about 15 minutes. Drain, let cool slightly, and then peel. Slice the potatoes and place in layers in a buttered 9 by 6-inch baking dish. In a mixing bowl, combine the sour cream, egg, milk, garlic, dill, salt, and pepper, and pour over the potatoes. Sprinkle the cheese over the top and bake in the oven for 10 minutes. Remove the potatoes while broiling the steaks (see below); then put the potatoes back on a lower shelf in the oven while cooking the steaks. The potatoes should cook a total of 25 to 30 minutes, until golden and bubbly.

Using 2 large nonstick sauté pans, heat 1 tablespoon of the oil in each. Sear the steaks in the pans over high heat for 1½ minutes per side; the steaks will still be rare. Remove the steaks and with a sharp knife, make deep diagonal gashes in the steaks about 1 inch apart. Spread

For the Sour Cream–Gratin Potatoes:

1¼ pounds russet potatoes
1 cup sour cream
1 egg, beaten
½ cup low-fat (2 percent) milk
1 teaspoon minced garlic
1 tablespoon minced dill
Salt and freshly ground black pepper to taste
1 cup shredded Monterey Jack cheese

For the Beef:

2 tablespoons olive oil

4 porterhouse steaks, 1 pound each and 1 inch thick

2 tablespoons softened butter

2 tablespoons Dijon mustard

Salt and freshly ground black pepper to taste

¾ cup brandy

1 tablespoon minced parsley

the butter on the steaks and into the gashes and then spread with the mustard. Season with salt and pepper and return the steaks to the pans. Sauté over medium-high heat for about 4 minutes on each side for medium-rare, 5 to 6 minutes for medium, or to desired doneness. Place the brandy in a small metal cup or dish and carefully ignite. When the flames from the brandy have died down, pour over the steaks. (Intrepid home cooks may pour the brandy into the pan and then ignite it; either way, take great care). Transfer the steaks to serving plates and garnish with the parsley.

Wine Suggestion: *Hermitage or Côte Rôtie from the Rhône Valley makes a great marriage with this steak recipe.*

In preparing this recipe, adapted with the permission of Little, Brown and Company from a recipe in *James Beard's American Cookery*, by James Beard (Boston: Little, Brown and Company, 1972), timing and organization are important. An alternative to flaming the brandy is to pour ½ cup sherry over the steaks before putting them in the oven.

MASALA SLOPPY JOES

Serves 4

Sloppy Joes—hamburger bun sandwiches filled with ground beef and onions in a tomato sauce—are, as the name implies, a little untidy to eat. In this recipe, we use pita pockets, which makes for neater and more convenient sandwiches. We further tweaked this American classic by using masala, the name for a wide variety of spice blends used in Indian cuisine. Here, we combine chile powder, black pepper, ground coriander, and turmeric in an aromatic masala, resulting in an altogether "grown-up" version of a favorite from childhood.

. . . .

Preheat the oven to 300 degrees.

Melt the butter in a large skillet. Add the onions and sauté over medium heat for 7 to 10 minutes, or until golden brown. Add the garlic and ginger and sauté for 2 to 3 minutes longer. Add the beef and cook for about 5 minutes or until just browned, using a kitchen fork to break up any lumps. Carefully pour off any fat in the pan.

Add the tomatoes, corn, pepper, chile powder, coriander, turmeric, and salt, and sauté for 3 to 4 minutes, stirring occasionally. Reduce the heat to low; add the beef stock and simmer for about 10 minutes, or until the mixture is moist but not soupy. In the meantime, wrap the pitas in aluminum foil and warm them in the oven. Remove the beef from the heat and season with salt and pepper.

To serve, squeeze some lime juice over the mango

3 tablespoons butter

2 onions, chopped

3 garlic cloves, minced

3 teaspoons minced ginger

1 pound lean high-quality ground beef

2 Roma tomatoes, chopped

¾ cup corn kernels (from 1 ear corn)

4 teaspoons freshly ground black pepper

1 tablespoon pure red chile powder

1 tablespoon ground coriander

½ teaspoon turmeric

Salt to taste

½ cup Beef Stock (page 200) or water

4 pita breads

½ lime

1 mango, peeled, pitted, and thinly sliced

slices and lay a few slices along the inside of the breads. Fill the pita "pockets" with large helpings of the Masala Sloppy Joe mixture.

WINE SUGGESTION: *Bardolino (Italy), Côtes du Rhône (France), or a Pinot Noir from the West Coast will successfully match the mixture of flavors in this recipe.*

Almost any chopped vegetables can be added to this dish; it's a great way to use up roasted or grilled leftovers. You can also use the beef mixture to fill samosas (page 14).

TROPICAL BEEF AND BANANA "PARFAIT" MEATLOAF WITH MASHED SWEET POTATOES AND MANGO–BLACK BEAN SALSA

Serves 4 to 6

This Caribbean-influenced meatloaf is composed in layers (including mashed banana) to resemble a parfait. It's another ideal spring dish that will put you in the mood for summer. The tropical salsa adds a cool, fruity counterpoint to the warm meatloaf and potatoes, but if you are short on time, you may omit it. If serving in summer, we recommend substituting a crisp green salad for the sweet potatoes.

....

To prepare the salsa, place all the ingredients in a mixing bowl and mix together gently. Chill in the refrigerator.

Preheat the oven to 375 degrees.

To prepare the meatloaf, place the beef, celery, 1 cup of the bread crumbs, salt, pepper, nutmeg, chile sauce, and eggs in a mixing bowl and combine thoroughly. Place half of the mixture in the bottom of a 9 by 6-inch loaf pan and smooth out evenly. Place the bananas in a clean bowl and mash together with the remaining bread crumbs and lime juice. Season with salt and pepper and spread over the meat in the pan. Sauté half of the bacon in a nonstick pan over medium-high heat for 2 to 3 minutes per side, or until cooked through. Drain on paper towels and place on top of the banana mixture in the pan. Top with the remaining beef mixture, spreading it out evenly, and lay the remaining (uncooked) strips of bacon on top of the beef. Bake in the oven for 50 minutes to 1 hour, or until the meatloaf is no longer pink on

FOR THE SALSA:

1½ cups drained cooked black beans

1 cup diced mango (from 2 small mangoes)

¼ cup finely diced red bell pepper

Juice of 1 lime

½ tablespoon habanero chile sauce (or other type of hot sauce), or to taste

Salt to taste

For the Meatloaf:

2 pounds lean high-
    quality ground beef
1½ stalks celery, finely
    diced (about 1 cup)
1½ cups dried seasoned
    bread crumbs
Salt and freshly ground
    black pepper to taste
⅛ teaspoon ground
    nutmeg
½ teaspoon habanero
    chile sauce (or other
    type of hot sauce), or
    to taste
2 eggs, beaten
3 fully ripe bananas
Juice of 1 lime
10 slices bacon, cut in
    half crosswise

For the Sweet Potatoes:

2 large sweet potatoes,
    about 2 pounds,
    peeled and chopped
2 tablespoons butter
2 tablespoons milk
Salt and freshly ground
    black pepper to taste
Pinch of ground nutmeg
    (optional)

the inside and the internal temperature reaches 160 degrees. Unmold onto a warm serving plate and cut into slices.

Meanwhile, place the sweet potatoes in a saucepan of salted water and bring to a boil. Continue to boil for about 20 minutes, until completely tender. Drain and place in a bowl with the butter, milk, salt, pepper, and nutmeg. Mash with a fork or electric whisk. Serve the meatloaf with the potatoes and salsa.

WINE SUGGESTION: *A late-harvest Zinfandel from California or a Merlot from St. Émilion (Bordeaux) or California will best match the sumptuous flavors.*

One cup of diced green apple (such as Granny Smith) can be substituted for the celery if you prefer. Its flavor will match the bacon well, but the texture will not be quite as crisp once it is cooked. If you can find them, yams will provide a more authentically Caribbean touch than sweet potatoes. Note that the internal temperature of the meatloaf will continue to rise by 5 to 10 degrees after it has been removed from the oven.

SWISS STEAK WITH HASHED POTATOES AND PARSNIPS

Serves 4

Swiss or "smothered" steak is a classic Midwestern American preparation that's a kissin' cousin to the Southern chicken-fried steak. "Swissing" refers to the process of pounding the steaks to make them more tender after they have been dredged in flour; the steaks are then braised in a hearty broth of stock and vegetables (or gravy, depending on family tradition). Although today's steaks are more tender than in the good old days when this dish originated, we still recommend a light pounding. The side dish of potatoes and parsnips is creamy, yet retains just enough chunky texture.

....

Pat the steaks dry and season with salt and pepper. Dredge the steaks in flour and pound them with the flat side of a meat cleaver or a rolling pin for about 30 seconds, to ensure that the flour adheres. Dredge the steaks once more in the flour and shake off any excess. Set aside.

Cook the bacon slices in a Dutch oven or large casserole dish over medium heat until all fat is rendered, about 3 minutes. Remove the bacon, chop, and reserve.

Add the steaks to the bacon drippings in the pan and cook over medium heat for about 5 minutes, turning once to brown on both sides. Remove the steaks and set aside. Turn down the heat and add the onions, carrots, celery, and garlic. Cover, and cook the vegetables for 10 minutes, or until the onions are translucent, stirring occasionally. (If necessary, add a little olive oil to prevent the vegetables from sticking.) Remove the lid, add the

For the Steaks:

4 top round steaks, choice grade, about 8 ounces each and ¾ inch thick

Salt and freshly ground black pepper to taste

½ cup all-purpose flour (or more, as needed)

2 slices bacon

3 onions, diced

3 carrots, diced

2 stalks celery, diced

2 garlic cloves, minced

Olive oil, if necessary

1 tablespoon tomato paste

1 bay leaf

4 sprigs thyme

½ cup beer

1 cup Beef Stock (page 200)

1 teaspoon minced lemon zest

For the Hashed Potatoes and Parsnips:

3 potatoes, peeled and quartered

4 parsnips, peeled and quartered

1 to 2 tablespoons butter

¼ to ½ cup light cream (as needed)

Salt and freshly ground white pepper to taste

tomato paste, bay leaf, and thyme to the pan, and cook for 5 minutes longer, stirring occasionally. Remove half of the vegetables and reserve.

Place the steaks on top of the vegetables remaining in the pan and add any juices that have been released from the meat. Sprinkle the bacon over the meat, and top with the reserved vegetables. Pour in the beer and beef stock and bring to a simmer on top of the stove. Turn down the heat, cover, and braise for 2 to 2½ hours, or until the steaks are tender enough to be pulled apart with a fork.

About 30 minutes before serving, prepare the hashed potatoes and parsnips. Put the potatoes and parsnips in a large saucepan and cover with cold salted water. Bring to a boil and simmer for 15 to 20 minutes, or until just tender. Drain the vegetables and return them to the saucepan. Place the pan over medium-low heat and let the vegetables dry for 2 to 3 minutes, shaking constantly. Turn the heat down to low, add the butter and ½ cup of cream, and break up the vegetables with a fork or potato masher until just slightly chunky. Add more cream if desired and season with salt and pepper to taste.

Remove the bay leaf and thyme sprigs from the Swiss steaks. Skim any fat from the surface and adjust the seasonings. Place the steaks on warm serving plates. Stir the lemon zest into the vegetables and spoon a large helping of vegetables over the steaks. Serve the hashed potatoes and parsnips on the side.

Adding lemon zest at the end of the recipe adds a bit of freshness, and helps to balance the richness of the broth. You can use chuck steak or bottom round for this recipe if you wish. If you prefer your potatoes (and parsnips) "mashed," simply whip them in a mixer, with an electric whisk, or pass them through a potato ricer before adding the butter and cream.

WINE SUGGESTION: *Petite Syrah from California or a French Côtes du Rhône to provide the dryness of character to complement the spicy flavors of this recipe.*

THAI BEEF SOUP WITH COCONUT, LEMONGRASS, AND NOODLES

Serves 4

This soup is inspired by a wonderful chef and restaurateur, Hubert Keller. Alsace-born Hubert owns Fleur de Lys, the superb French restaurant in San Francisco, and he is one of the most well-liked and respected individuals in the industry. Hubert has a similar recipe featuring lobster and shrimp, without the noodles included here. The meaty texture of the seafood and the Thai flavors are an exciting combination; our uncommon variation is one of the lightest-flavored beef dishes you'll find.

....

Place the beef in a mixing bowl, add the soy sauce and sesame oil, and let marinate at room temperature for 2 to 3 hours, or at least 30 minutes, turning occasionally.

To prepare the soup base, place the coconut milk in a large saucepan. Cut the lemongrass in half across and then in half lengthwise. Crush with the back of a heavy knife and add to the pan. Add the ginger, lime leaves, celery, lemon juice, garlic, cilantro, wine, salt, and pepper, and bring to a boil, stirring occasionally. Boil gently for 5 minutes and then remove from the heat and let infuse, covered, while cooking the beef and vegetables.

Heat a dry wok or cast-iron skillet over high heat. Add the beef and marinade and sear for 8 to 10 minutes, stirring constantly, or until the beef is tender, browned, and the liquid has evaporated. Remove the beef and pat dry with paper towels.

To prepare the vegetables, blanch the tomatoes in a

For the Beef:
1 pound skirt steak, cut across the grain into pieces 1 inch long and $\frac{1}{8}$ inch thick
2 tablespoons soy sauce
2 tablespoons toasted sesame oil

For the Soup Base:

3 cans (14 ounces each)
   coconut milk
3 stalks lemongrass,
   tough outer leaves
   removed
3 tablespoons minced
   ginger
3 kaffir lime leaves, or 1
   teaspoon lemon zest
1 stalk celery, diced
   (about ½ cup)
¼ cup freshly squeezed
   lemon juice
2 teaspoons minced
   garlic
¼ cup minced cilantro
1 cup dry white wine
Salt and freshly ground
   white pepper to taste

For the Vegetables and Noodles:

3 Roma tomatoes
1 tablespoon olive oil
1 sweet onion, finely
   sliced
3 scallions, finely sliced
1 carrot, finely sliced
5 ounces dry rice
   noodles (or jasmine
   rice noodles)
½ cup finely sliced basil

small saucepan of boiling water for 2 minutes. Drain, and when cool enough to handle, peel, cut in half, and gently squeeze out the seeds. Dice the tomatoes and set aside. Heat the olive oil in a saucepan, add the onion, scallions, and carrot, and sauté over medium-high heat for 2 minutes.

Strain the coconut liquid into the saucepan and bring to a boil. Add the noodles and cook for about 5 minutes, or until tender. Add the basil, blanched tomatoes, and cooked beef, and season to taste. Ladle into serving bowls.

WINE SUGGESTION: *For a soup so abundantly spiced, a light acidic wine is recommended, such as a Spanish Rioja, Italian Bardolino, Californian Petite Syrah, or a Tavel Rosé from the Rhône Valley.*

The rice noodles are available in the Asian foods section of most supermarkets. Lemongrass is becoming more widely available in supermarket produce sections, and can also be found in most Asian markets.

FILET MIGNON IN A WHISKEY PAN SAUCE WITH MUSHROOMS AND POTATO-LEEK SQUARES

Serves 4

FOR THE POTATO-LEEK
SQUARES:

1½ pounds Yukon Gold
   potatoes, peeled and
   thinly sliced

8 ounces leeks (or
   scallions), white part
   only, thinly sliced

⅓ cup olive oil

Salt and freshly ground
   black pepper to taste

FOR THE MUSHROOMS:

2 tablespoons butter

12 ounces mushrooms,
   sliced

2 teaspoons all-purpose
   flour

Salt and pepper to taste

1 cup heavy cream,
   warmed

Here's another beef recipe that the late James Beard wrote for Omaha Steaks a few years back. It pairs the rich beef filet with earthy tones of mushrooms and whiskey. We've matched Jim's classic with a simple yet delicious side of potatoes and leeks. The mushroom accompaniment is wonderful, but slightly high in calories, so by all means omit it if this is a concern.

. . . .

Preheat the oven to 350 degrees. Place the potatoes, leeks, and olive oil in a mixing bowl and season with salt and pepper. Gently toss to mix well. Transfer to a 6 by 9-inch baking dish and pat gently to form an even layer. Cover the dish with foil and bake in the oven for 1½ hours or until the potatoes are tender. Let cool completely, cover with plastic wrap, and chill. When ready to serve, preheat the oven to 450 degrees. Cut the potatoes into 4 even sections. Using a metal spatula, transfer the squares to a rimmed baking sheet. Bake in the oven for 30 minutes or until the tops are browned.

To prepare the mushrooms, melt the butter in a saucepan and sauté the mushrooms over medium-high heat for about 5 minutes or until lightly golden. Add the flour, season with salt and pepper, and stir well. Stir in the cream and keep warm.

To prepare the steaks, melt the 1 tablespoon butter in a sauté pan or cast-iron skillet. Season the filets with salt and pepper. When the pan is hot, sear the filets over high heat for 2½ to 3 minutes on each side for medium-rare, about 4 minutes on each side for medium, or to the desired doneness. Remove the steaks from the pan and just before serving, stir the whiskey into the pan juices. Bring to a boil and cook for 2 minutes or until the alcohol burns off.

In a separate sauté pan, melt the 4 tablespoons of butter and sauté the bread slices over medium-high heat, turning often so the bread becomes crispy and not soggy, about 3 or 4 minutes. Transfer to a serving platter, top with the filets, and arrange the mushrooms in the center. Spoon the whiskey sauce over the filets and serve with the potatoes.

WINE SUGGESTION: *The finest Pinot Noir or French Burgundy you can afford will do this recipe justice.*

> Yukon Gold are the potatoes of choice here because they are less starchy and give this side a better, crispier texture. For the same reason, new potatoes would also work well.

FOR THE STEAKS:
1 tablespoon butter
4 filet mignons, prime or
    choice grade, 6 ounces
    each
Salt and freshly ground
    black pepper to taste
½ cup Scotch whiskey

4 tablespoons butter
4 slices French bread

PICADILLO-STUFFED RED BELL PEPPERS WITH ALMOND RICE

Serves 4

FOR THE PICADILLO:

½ cup sherry

½ cup raisins

2 tablespoons vegetable
  oil

1 onion, chopped

2 garlic cloves, minced

1 pound lean high-
  quality ground beef

1 teaspoon ground
  cumin

Pinch of ground cloves

1 (2-inch) cinnamon stick

4 Roma tomatoes,
  blanched (page 207),
  peeled, seeded, and
  diced

½ cup Beef Stock (page
  200) or water

½ cup bottled green
  olives stuffed with
  pimento, sliced

Salt and freshly ground
  black pepper to taste

Beef-stuffed peppers are an all-American standby, but this recipe uses a sweet and savory Mexican-style picadillo filling. Picadillo is customarily made with beef or pork, tomatoes, onions, and raisins; sometimes it also contains herbs, olives, and/or dried chile slivers. Toasted almonds are often included, but we have added them to the rice here. However, if you prefer to serve plain rice with the stuffed peppers, add ¼ cup toasted almonds to the picadillo after it has finished cooking. The picadillo can be made up to 2 days in advance and refrigerated until needed.

To prepare the picadillo, place the sherry in a cup, add the raisins, and let them plump until needed. Heat the vegetable oil in a large skillet. Add the onion and sauté over medium heat for 7 or 8 minutes, or until golden. Add the garlic and sauté for 2 to 3 minutes longer. Add the beef and cook about 5 minutes or until just browned, using a fork to break up any lumps. Pour off any excess fat from the pan. Add the cumin, cloves, cinnamon, and tomatoes, and sauté for 3 to 4 minutes, stirring occasionally. Turn the heat down to low, add the beef stock, sherry, raisins, olives, salt, and pepper. Stir well and simmer the picadillo for 20 to 25 minutes, or until most of the liquid has evaporated. Remove from the heat, let cool slightly, and season with salt and pepper to taste.

While the picadillo is cooking, prepare the rice. Heat

the butter and oil in a heavy saucepan over medium heat. When the butter begins to sizzle, add the onion and sauté for about 5 minutes, until translucent. Add the rice and continue to sauté while stirring for 2 to 3 minutes until all the rice is coated. Raise the heat, pour in the chicken stock, season with salt and pepper, and bring to a boil. Reduce to a simmer, cover the pan, and cook over low heat until the rice has absorbed all the liquid, about 15 minutes. Remove the rice from the heat and let it rest, covered, for about 5 minutes. Fluff the rice with a fork while adding the ¼ cup toasted almonds.

While the rice is cooking, cut off the top of each bell pepper and discard. Carefully rinse out the seeds and cut or tear out any ribs and membranes without damaging the outside of the pepper. Fill the peppers with the picadillo.

To serve, spoon the rice in a ring around the plate. Place the stuffed pepper in the center of the rice and garnish with the cilantro sprigs. Sprinkle the toasted almonds over the rice pilaf.

WINE SUGGESTION: *Rioja or Penedès reds from Spain will best complement this food, or a Petite Syrah from California.*

FOR THE ALMOND RICE:
2 tablespoons butter
1 tablespoon olive oil
1 small onion, chopped
1 cup long-grain white rice
2 cups chicken stock
Salt and freshly ground white pepper to taste
¼ cup blanched slivered almonds, toasted and chopped (page 210)

FOR THE PEPPERS:
4 large red bell peppers, roasted and peeled (page 208)

4 sprigs cilantro, for garnish
¼ cup blanched slivered almonds, toasted and chopped (page 210)

Roasted bell peppers impart a deliciously smoky accent to this dish. Fresh bell peppers may be used instead; they actually hold up better in the cooking process and are more manageable, but they will not add the same flavor. After stuffing them with the picadillo, bake at 350 degrees, covered, for about 30 minutes, until the peppers are tender but still hold their shape. Roasted poblanos may be used if you prefer a more fiery dish; slit along their side to stuff; handle carefully, as they tear more easily than bell peppers.

GRILLED BONELESS STRIP STEAKS WITH MERLOT SAUCE, NEW POTATOES, AND WILTED GARLICKY SPINACH

Serves 4

FOR THE SAUCE:

2 tablespoons olive oil

4 garlic cloves, minced

1 cup diced onion

1 cup sliced carrot

1 cup chopped celery

3 bay leaves

1 teaspoon black
   peppercorns

2 tablespoons sugar

¼ teaspoon salt

3 cups Merlot wine
   (about ¾ bottle)

3 cups Beef Stock (page
   200)

The flavor of the strip steaks is perfectly complemented in this recipe by the intense wine sauce. If you enjoy wine, you might like to experiment with the sauce by using different types; good alternatives include Cabernet, Chianti, or Rioja. It's a sure sign that spring is here when new potatoes are in the markets, and their delicate flavor is well suited to the subtle tones that the mint imparts. At other times of year, substitute Yellow Finn or small Yukon Gold potatoes.

· ·

To prepare the sauce, heat the olive oil in a saucepan. Add the garlic, onion, carrot, celery, bay leaves, and peppercorns and sauté over medium heat for 7 or 8 minutes, until the vegetables are well softened. Add the sugar and caramelize the vegetables for 2 to 3 minutes, stirring frequently. Season with the salt, stir in the wine, and cook at a low boil until the liquid is reduced by two-thirds (about 40 minutes). Add the stock and reduce by two-thirds again (35 to 40 minutes longer). Strain through a fine-mesh strainer into a clean saucepan and continue to reduce the sauce until about 1 cup remains and it is thick enough to coat the back of a spoon.

Place the potatoes and mint in a saucepan of cold salted water. Bring to a boil and simmer for about 12 minutes or until tender when pierced with a knife. Drain, cut in half, and dot with the butter so they are coated when it melts. When ready to serve, garnish with the parsley.

Season the steaks with salt and pepper. Heat the oil in a heavy cast-iron skillet over high heat until the oil begins to smoke. Add the steaks to the hot pan and sear on the first side for about 4 minutes. Turn over and sear for 3 to 4 minutes for medium rare. Cook for 1 to 2 minutes longer on each side for medium, or cook to desired doneness.

While the steaks are cooking, prepare the spinach. Heat the olive oil in a sauté pan, add the garlic, and sauté for 2 minutes, until softened. Add the spinach and sauté, while tossing, for 2 minutes longer, until wilted. Season with salt and pepper.

Ladle the sauce onto warm serving plates, place the steak on the sauce, and serve with potatoes and spinach.

WINE SUGGESTION: *The same Merlot used in the sauce (preferably from California) will work best; or try a late-vintage Cabernet from Italy or a Rioja from Spain, as these will also complement the spices used in this recipe.*

If you prefer, use chard or red chard instead of spinach.

FOR THE POTATOES:

8 new potatoes (about 1¼ pounds), cleaned thoroughly

4 sprigs mint

2 tablespoons butter, diced

1 teaspoon chopped parsley, for garnish

FOR THE STEAKS:

4 boneless strip steaks, prime or choice grade, 10 ounces each

Salt and freshly ground black pepper to taste

2 tablespoons olive oil

FOR THE WILTED SPINACH:

2 tablespoons olive oil

3 garlic cloves, minced

1 pound spinach, well washed and stemmed

Salt and freshly ground black pepper to taste

ROAST BEEF AND YORKSHIRE PUDDING WITH ROAST POTATOES AND MRS. H'S PERFECT GRAVY

Serves 4

FOR THE ROAST BEEF:

2 tablespoons olive oil

4 pounds standing prime
   rib roast, bone in,
   trimmed close to the
   "eye," with feather
   bones removed

Salt and freshly ground
   black pepper to taste

FOR THE VEGETABLES:

8 carrots

8 potatoes (about 4
   ounces each), peeled

4 parsnips, peeled

This dish is the quintessential English Sunday lunch. But, as co-author John Harrisson, born and raised in the English heartland, points out, this is also a special occasion dish, one he loves to prepare for friends and family at Eastertime. Yorkshire pudding, made with a pancake-like batter, is a revered British tradition; originally, it was served with gravy before the beef course but it has long been the accompaniment of choice for roast beef. Because of its close similarity to American popovers, "Yorky Pud" (as it is affectionately known) is ideally prepared using popover molds. Alternatively, the batter can be poured directly into the roasting pan with the beef, after most of the drippings have been poured out. Although it will not rise as delicately as when cooked in its own pan, the flavor is still wonderful.

Preheat the oven to 425 degrees.

To prepare the beef, heat the oil in a cast-iron skillet or heavy sauté pan. When almost smoking, sear the beef on each side for 3 minutes. Season all over with salt and pepper and transfer the beef (fat side up) and drippings to a roasting pan large enough to also accommodate the vegetables later. Cover the pan with foil and place in the middle of the oven. Roast for 15 minutes and then turn down the oven temperature to 400 degrees. Baste the beef with the drippings and return to the oven. The vegetables need to be added to the pan about 50 minutes before the beef is done, so plan accordingly. At the

FOR THE YORKSHIRE PUDDING:
¾ cup all-purpose flour
½ teaspoon salt
⅛ teaspoon nutmeg
1 egg, beaten
1¼ cups milk

FOR THE GRAVY:
2 tablespoons beef
  drippings and
  sediment
1 tablespoon all-purpose
  flour
1½ cups hot Beef Stock
  (page 200)
1 tablespoon port

1 recipe Horseradish
  Cream (page 178), or
  prepared horseradish
  or mustard (optional)
4 sprigs sage, for garnish
  (optional)

appropriate time, place them around the beef, baste with the drippings, and cover the pan again before returning to the oven. For rare beef, roast for an additional hour after reducing the oven temperature (1 hour, 15 minutes total); for medium-rare, roast 1 hour and 15 minutes after reducing the oven temperature (1 hour and 30 minutes total); for medium, roast for 1 hour and 30 minutes after reducing the oven temperature (a total of 1 hour and 45 minutes). You may, of course, roast the beef further, according to your personal preference. Remove from the oven and let the beef rest on a carving board for 5 minutes before slicing. Reserve the drippings in the pan for gravy.

Prepare the Yorkshire pudding batter 1 hour before you are ready to serve. Sift the flour, salt, and nutmeg into a mixing bowl and create a well in the center. Add the egg and a little of the milk to the well, and begin whisking. Gradually add the rest of the milk and whisk until the batter has a smooth consistency. Let stand for 30 minutes. Place 2 tablespoons of the hot beef drippings in a 6-inch square baking pan, or into popover molds, or the molds of a cupcake pan. Heat the pan on the top rack of the oven and when it begins to smoke, add the batter. Cook for 35 to 40 minutes if using the square pan or 15 to 20 minutes if using individual molds, or until golden brown and crisp with a creamy-looking (but cooked) center. Do not open the oven door until at least the minimum cooking time or the puddings will fall. If using the square pan, cut the pudding into 4 portions.

Prepare the gravy while the beef is resting. Pour 2 tablespoons of the beef drippings and sediment into a small saucepan set over medium heat. Whisk in the flour, add the beef stock and port, and bring just to a boil, while stirring. Simmer for 2 minutes while stirring and transfer to a gravy boat.

Serve the beef with the vegetables, Yorkshire pudding, gravy, and horseradish. Garnish the plate with the sage.

WINE SUGGESTION: *Cabernet Sauvignon (from France, Italy, or Australia) or a Pinot Noir from the West Coast have the character needed for a fine roast beef.*

Roasts can vary significantly in size, and the important thing is to allow about 15 minutes per pound plus 15 minutes total cooking time for rare-cooked; 18 minutes per pound plus 18 minutes for medium-rare; and 20 minutes per pound plus 20 minutes for medium. Covering the roasting pan not only keeps the oven clean but also keeps the beef moist and helps prevent the drippings from burning up. Removing the foil for the last 15 minutes of cooking will give the roast an attractive crispness.

BREAKFAST-IN-BED STEAK AND EGGS WITH SALSA FRESCA
Serves 4

Treat Mom to a special breakfast on her special day—or prepare this recipe for a Cinco de Mayo brunch celebration. If the little ones are helping fix breakfast for Mom, let them mash the lemon-garlic butter and supervise them while they make the salsa. Grown-ups should *not* delegate the tasks of frying the tortilla strips or mincing the jalapeño! This recipe can easily be scaled up (or down) to accommodate any size family.

· ·

Thoroughly combine all the salsa ingredients in a mixing bowl. Add a little more sugar if the tomatoes are underripe, but take care that the salsa does not taste too sweet. Chill the salsa in the refrigerator for at least 30 minutes before serving to allow the flavors to marry.

To prepare the tortilla strips, pour enough oil into a deep-fryer or saucepan to come 2 or 3 inches up the sides and heat to 350 degrees. Cut the tortillas into ⅛-inch-wide strips; cut the longer strips in half. Add the tortilla strips to the oil and fry in batches for 2 to 3 minutes or until golden brown (frying in batches will ensure the strips do not crowd the pan and significantly lower the temperature of the oil). Remove with a slotted spoon, drain on paper towels, and season with salt.

Combine the ingredients for the lemon-garlic butter in a bowl and mash to incorporate. Melt 3 tablespoons of the lemon-garlic butter in a heavy skillet set over medium-high heat. Season the steaks with salt and pep-

FOR THE SALSA FRESCA:

3 tablespoons finely diced sweet onion

1 pound Roma tomatoes, diced

1 jalapeño chile, finely diced

2 tablespoons finely chopped cilantro leaves

¾ teaspoon sugar

¾ teaspoon salt

1 tablespoon freshly squeezed lime juice

FOR THE TORTILLA STRIPS:

1 quart vegetable oil, for deep-frying

3 or 4 small corn tortillas

Salt to taste

For the Lemon-Garlic Butter:

3 tablespoons butter, softened

1½ tablespoons Worcestershire sauce

½ tablespoon freshly squeezed lemon juice

2 garlic cloves, minced

For the Steaks:

4 boneless strip steaks, about 7 ounces each and ¾ inch thick

Salt and freshly ground black pepper to taste

For the Eggs:

2 tablespoons butter

8 eggs

Salt and pepper to taste

per, and when the butter is sizzling in the skillet, add the steaks. Sear for 1½ minutes on each side; turn the heat down to medium and sauté the steaks for 1 to 2 minutes on each side for medium-rare, 2 to 3 minutes for medium, or to desired doneness. Keep warm.

To cook the eggs, melt 1 tablespoon of the butter in a large nonstick saucepan over medium heat (you will need 2 tablespoons of butter if you are using a pan that does not have a nonstick surface). When the butter begins to bubble, gently add 4 of the eggs, one by one, and season with salt and pepper (cook the eggs in 2 batches, depending on the size of the pan). Take care to keep the yolks intact as you add the eggs to the pan. Cook the eggs, covered, until the whites are firm and the yolks are just beginning to set, about 4 or 5 minutes. Remove and keep warm. Melt the remaining 1 tablespoon of butter in the pan before cooking the second batch of eggs.

To serve, place the steaks to one side of each warm serving plate and top each steak with 1 teaspoon of the remaining lemon-garlic butter. Gently place 2 of the eggs on the other side of each plate, taking care not to break the yolks. Spoon a generous portion of the salsa down the center of the plate, overlapping the eggs and the steak. Top with a heaping pile of tortilla strips and serve immediately.

To make your morning run smoother, slice the tortillas and prepare the lemon-garlic butter and salsa a day ahead. You can fry the tortilla strips a day ahead if you keep them tightly covered and dry.

This recipe is for sunny-side-up eggs. If you prefer your eggs over-easy, cook them as for sunny-side-up eggs but without covering them, and then gently turn them over, and cook on the other side for another minute, just to set. Most people have long-established fried egg preferences, so it is best to take requests before beginning to cook. Scrambled eggs taste just as great here, and are easier to prepare for large groups and/or with kids.

WINE SUGGESTION: *This recipe inspires the selection of a robust French Burgundy or a Pinot Noir from the American West Coast.*

ROASTED GARLIC MUSTARD–GLAZED T-BONE STEAKS AND SPICY ONION RINGS WITH CORN AND SHIITAKE MUSHROOM SALSA

Serves 4

Like Mother's Day, this is one special occasion when many families try to pull out all the stops to make sure that a loved parent knows he is appreciated—and that he does not go hungry! Most dads we know love steaks, especially when they have assertive flavors and come grilled. Most dads also go for onion rings, and these will not disappoint them. A lot of testing went in to getting them right: We tried red onions, but they did not crisp up as well. We recommend not using the innermost rings of the onions as they are hard to separate and get gluey and heavy with too much flour; use them for other recipes.

· ·

To prepare the salsa, heat a nonstick pan, add half of the corn, and dry-roast over high heat until dark, tossing constantly, about 5 or 6 minutes. Remove and let cool. Repeat for the remaining corn (cooking in 2, or even 3 batches avoids overcrowding the pan). Clean out the pan with a paper towel, add 2 or 3 teaspoons of the olive oil to the pan, and sauté the mushrooms until well cooked, 3 to 4 minutes. Remove and let cool. In a mixing bowl, combine the corn, mushrooms, and the remaining salsa ingredients. Set aside.

Prepare the grill (alternatively the steaks can be pan-fried). To prepare the glaze, mash the roasted garlic in a mixing bowl to form a paste. Add the remaining glaze ingredients and combine thoroughly.

For the Corn and Shiitake Salsa:

3 cups fresh corn kernels (from 4 ears)

3 tablespoons olive oil

8 ounces shiitake mushrooms, chopped

2 poblano chiles, roasted, peeled, seeded, and diced (page 208)

2 roasted garlic cloves (page 206)

2 tablespoons chopped oregano

2 teaspoons adobo sauce (from canned chipotles)

½ tablespoon sherry vinegar

1 teaspoon freshly squeezed lime juice

1 teaspoon ground cumin

For the Roasted Garlic Mustard Glaze:

6 roasted garlic cloves
   (page 206)
6 tablespoons Dijon
   mustard
2 tablespoons dark
   brown sugar
4 teaspoons apple cider
   vinegar
½ tablespoon
   Worcestershire sauce
¼ teaspoon cayenne

For the Spicy Onion Rings:

1 cup all-purpose flour
½ cup cornstarch
1 tablespoon pure red
   chile powder
½ teaspoon cayenne
1 teaspoon ground
   cumin
¼ teaspoon salt
½ teaspoon freshly
   ground black pepper
1 quart vegetable oil, for
   deep-frying
4 large onions, thinly
   sliced, rings separated

To prepare the onion rings, thoroughly combine the flour, cornstarch, chile powder, cayenne, cumin, salt, and pepper in a large mixing bowl. Pour enough oil into a deep-fryer or saucepan to come 2 or 3 inches up the sides and heat to 350 degrees. Toss the onion rings in the dry mixture and gently shake off any excess. Use tongs to carefully place some of the coated onions in the hot oil; fry until crispy and golden brown, 2 to 3 minutes. Fry the onions in 3 or 4 batches, so they do not crowd the pan. Remove the onions with a slotted spoon and drain on paper towels. Season with additional salt to taste and keep warm.

Season the steaks with salt and pepper. Grill the steaks on the first side for 4 or 5 minutes, or until well seared and grill-marked. Turn the steaks over and brush about 2 tablespoons of the glaze on the grilled side of the steak. Grill for 4 to 5 minutes longer for medium-rare, 5 to 6 minutes per side for medium, or to the desired doneness. Before removing the steaks from the grill, spread the remaining glaze over them.

To serve, place the steaks glazed side up in the center of warm serving plates. Pile the onion rings on top of the steaks and serve the salsa on the side.

WINE SUGGESTION: *Spanish or Italian reds will match the flavors of this dish, preferably Cabernet blends, Chianti Classico, or Barbaresco.*

The trick with preparing the onion rings is to maintain the oil at 350 degrees during cooking. When the temperature drops below that, the onion rings take longer to cook, absorb too much oil, and do not crisp properly. If you have more than one set of hands, prepare the onion rings and steak at the same time. If not, have the onion rings ready to fry as soon as the steaks come off the grill.

The adobo sauce used in the salsa is the liquid in which canned chipotle chiles are packed. You can substitute another chile sauce or paste if you prefer.

FOR THE STEAKS:

4 T-bone steaks, prime or choice grade, about 1 pound each, 1 to 1¼ inches thick

Salt and freshly ground black pepper to taste

2. RECIPES FOR SUMMER

Recipes for Special Occasions

**Thai Beef Salad in a Beefsteak
Tomato, page 64**

JOHN SEDLAR'S "JIMI HENDRIX STEAK EXPERIENCE"

Serves 6

As you might be able to tell from the title of this recipe, John Sedlar is one of America's most creative chefs. He is also one of the pioneers of modern Southwestern cuisine, although this particular recipe hardly falls into this category. Instead, this dish was inspired by a menu he wrote for Billboard Live, a rock-and-roll supper club on Sunset Boulevard in Hollywood, California; many of the dishes were inspired by famous musicians. With this presentation, featuring the bright psychedelic colors of the beet syrup and cilantro, you get a Hendrix-style purple and bright green haze on the plates!

To prepare the marinade, place the oil, vinegar, garlic, and peppercorns in a dish or mixing bowl and whisk to combine. Add the tarragon and rosemary. Add the steaks, coating with the marinade on both sides, and let marinate in the refrigerator overnight.

To prepare the beet syrup, place the beet juice in a small saucepan and bring to a boil. Cook over medium-high heat for 15 to 20 minutes, or until syrupy in consistency and ¼ cup remains. Lightly season with salt and pepper.

To prepare the cilantro oil, blanch 3 bunches of cilantro in boiling water for 10 seconds. Remove and shock in a bowl of ice water to stop the cooking process. Transfer to a blender with the remaining bunches of uncooked cilantro and puree while slowly adding the olive oil. Let the mixture rest overnight. The next day,

FOR THE MARINADE AND STEAKS:

½ cup olive oil

¼ cup balsamic vinegar

2 tablespoons pureed or finely minced garlic

2 tablespoons black peppercorns

3 sprigs tarragon, leaves removed and coarsely chopped

3 sprigs rosemary, leaves removed and coarsely chopped

6 portions of skirt steak, select grade or better, about 8 ounces each, or top sirloin steaks, prime or choice grade, lightly pounded to a thickness of ½ inch

FOR THE BEET SYRUP:

1 cup beet juice

Salt and freshly ground black pepper to taste

For the Cilantro Oil:

6 bunches cilantro, thick
    stems removed
1 cup olive oil
Salt and pepper to taste

For the Dressing and Salad:

½ cup vegetable oil
2 tablespoons Dijon
    mustard
½ cup red wine vinegar
1 teaspoon salt
1 teaspoon freshly
    ground black pepper
6 bunches watercress,
    washed and drained

strain through cheesecloth into an attractive glass bottle and season with salt and pepper.

Prepare the grill.

To prepare the dressing, whisk together the vegetable oil and mustard in a mixing bowl. Whisk in the vinegar and season with the salt and pepper. Let chill in the refrigerator. Remove the thick stems of the watercress and chill the leaves. When ready to serve, toss the watercress with the dressing and pile in a high mound on the center of each serving plate, leaving plenty of room around the watercress.

Remove the steaks from the marinade and grill over medium-high heat for 2 to 2½ minutes on each side for medium-rare, about 3 minutes on each side for medium, or to desired doneness.

Slice each steak and arrange on top of the salad. Drizzle or spoon the cilantro oil and beet syrup around the salad in attractive or free-form psychedelic patterns.

WINE SUGGESTION: *Zinfandel from California, Cabernet Sauvignon from California, or Chianti Classico from Italy will perfectly complement the combination of seasonings and steaks.*

Not only should the steaks marinate overnight, but the cilantro oil should also be prepared a day in advance to give the ingredients time to infuse and settle. You can juice the beets yourself or buy beet juice at a health food store. For the best visual effect, serve this dish on large white serving plates.

PACIFIC RIM BEEF STIR-FRY WITH WONTON STRIPS

Serves 4

This "fusion" recipe combines a Szechuan-style stir-fry containing the flavors of hoisin sauce and chile bean paste with Japanese mirin (a sweet, thick rice wine) Indonesian chile sauce (Sambal Oelek), and Thai-style jasmine rice. Some cooks may question the idea of dishes containing chile sauce in summertime, but like many Americans, we enjoy the flavor and piquancy of chiles anytime. We also like the theory that chiles are particularly popular in countries with warm climates because their heat induces sweating, which in turn cools the body. For this recipe, use thin asparagus spears; if they are thick, cut them in half lengthwise.

. . . .

Place the beef in a mixing bowl, add the soy sauce and sesame oil, and let marinate at room temperature for 30 minutes, turning occasionally.

Meanwhile, bring a saucepan of salted water to a boil and blanch the asparagus for 2 minutes. Drain and reserve the asparagus. Heat a wok or large sauté pan over high heat and add the peanut oil. Add the beef and 1 tablespoon of the sherry, stir-fry until the beef separates, and reduce the heat to medium. When the liquid has evaporated and the beef is dry, about 4 or 5 minutes, add the black bean paste, hoisin sauce, garlic, salt, and mirin, and the remaining 1 tablespoon of sherry. Stir to combine thoroughly, and increase the heat to high. Add the carrot, celery, reserved blanched asparagus, and stir

For the Garnish:
Peanut oil
2 wonton wrappers (3½
    inches square) or 1
    large egg roll wrapper
    (6½ inches square), cut
    into strips
4 sprigs cilantro
2 cups Jasmine Rice
    (page 202)

For the Beef and
Marinade:
1 pound skirt steak,
    select grade or better,
    cut into thin strips
    about 2 inches long
    and ¼ inch thick
2 tablespoons soy sauce
2 tablespoons toasted
    sesame oil

FOR THE STIR-FRY:

1 bunch asparagus, top 3
    inches of the spears
    only
2 tablespoons peanut oil
2 tablespoons dry sherry
2 tablespoons black bean
    paste
1 tablespoon hoisin
    sauce
2 garlic cloves, minced
½ teaspoon salt
1 tablespoon mirin (or
    brown sugar)
1 large carrot, finely
    julienned (about 1
    cup)
2 stalks celery, finely
    julienned (about 1
    cup)
2 scallions, finely sliced
2 teaspoons minced
    ginger
½ teaspoon freshly
    ground Szechuan or
    black pepper
1 teaspoon chile sauce
    with garlic (such as
    Sambal Oelek), or your
    favorite hot sauce

well. Add the scallions, ginger, pepper, and chile sauce, and stir-fry until thoroughly combined.

For the garnish, heat ½ inch of peanut oil in a skillet until almost smoking. Add the wonton strips and fry for 30 seconds or until golden brown and crispy. Garnish the stir-fry with the wonton strips and the cilantro and serve with the rice.

WINE SUGGESTION: *A hearty Pinot Noir from the West Coast.*

If you prefer, use a plain long-grain rice (page 205) instead of the jasmine rice.

SIRLOIN STEAKS WITH SUMMER VEGETABLE GRATIN AND RED CHILE MASHED POTATOES

Serves 4

FOR THE RED CHILE MASHED POTATOES:

1½ pounds potatoes, peeled and chopped

2 tablespoons butter

1 cup milk

3 garlic cloves, minced

1½ cups fresh corn kernels (from 2 ears)

½ tablespoon pure red chile powder

½ tablespoon chopped cilantro

1 teaspoon honey

Salt to taste

This summery "meat and two vegetable" dish is both versatile and filling. For a cooler side dish, easier to make ahead, you can substitute Kathy's Potato Salad (page 96). You can substitute boneless strip steaks or filet mignons for the hearty sirloin steaks, and you can broil them if you prefer or finish them in the pan. Likewise, the vegetables for the gratin can be sautéed instead of grilled.

....

Prepare the grill.

Place the potatoes in a saucepan of salted water and bring to a boil. Turn down the heat and simmer for about 20 minutes, until tender. Drain and transfer to a mixing bowl. Meanwhile, in a sauté pan, melt the butter with the milk, bring to a boil, and add the garlic and corn. Turn down the heat and simmer for 3 minutes. Sprinkle in the chile powder and stir. Strain the mixture, reserving the corn separately from the liquid. With an electric mixer (or with a wire whisk), whip the potatoes while drizzling in the reserved cooking liquid, adding a little more milk as needed. Stir in the reserved corn, the cilantro and honey, and season with salt.

While the potatoes are cooking, prepare the gratin. Place the olive oil in a glass dish or a mixing bowl and add the zucchini, yellow squash, tomato, onion, eggplant, and garlic. Coat with the oil and then place the vegetables on the grill, starting with the eggplant slices closest to the middle, followed by the onion, squash, zucchini, and tomato slices, in that order, so that the vegetables that take the longest to cook will take the most heat. Grill the vegetables for 8 to 10 minutes on each side or until tender. When cool enough to handle, slice the zucchini and squash into half-moons. Transfer the grilled vegetables to an 8-inch square ovenproof glass baking dish, layering the vegetables evenly. Grill the bell pepper on all sides until blackened and transfer to a mixing bowl. Cover the bowl with plastic wrap and let the pepper "steam" for 10 minutes. Peel off the blackened skin with a knife, remove the seeds, and cut the pepper into quarters. Place on top of the vegetables in the baking dish. Mix the cheeses together in a bowl, and sprinkle over the vegetables. Set aside.

Preheat the oven broiler. Season the steaks with salt and pepper, heat the oil in a cast-iron skillet and sear the steaks over high heat for 1 minute on each side. Transfer to the grill and cook for 3 minutes per side for medium-rare, about 4 minutes per side for medium, or to desired doneness. Transfer to serving plates. Place the vegetables under the broiler and cook until the cheese melts and turns golden, 2 to 3 minutes. Serve the steaks with the potatoes and vegetable gratin.

WINE SUGGESTION: *Rhône Valley reds such as Châteauneuf-du-Pape or Crozes-Hermitage, or a West Coast Pinot Noir, all work well.*

By all means substitute your favorite vegetables (or whatever is in season) for those suggested in the gratin recipe. If you wish, use ⅔ cup of just one type of cheese for the gratin topping.

FOR THE SUMMER
VEGETABLE GRATIN:
½ cup olive oil
2 small zucchini, cut in
    half lengthwise
2 small yellow squash,
    cut in half lengthwise
1 large tomato (8 to 10
    ounces), sliced ½ inch
    thick
1 sweet onion, sliced ½
    inch thick
1 small eggplant (10 to 12
    ounces), sliced ½ inch
    thick
1 teaspoon minced garlic
1 large red bell pepper
⅓ cup grated mozzarella
    cheese
⅓ cup grated Monterey
    Jack cheese

FOR THE STEAKS:
4 top sirloin steaks,
    about 8 ounces each,
    1¼ inches thick, prime
    or choice grade
Salt and freshly ground
    black pepper
1 tablespoon olive oil

STEAK SANDWICH WITH WILD MUSHROOMS AND SHALLOTS

Serves 4

1 recipe Shoestring
   Potatoes (page 17)

FOR THE MUSHROOMS
AND SHALLOTS:
1 tablespoon olive oil
10 shallots, finely sliced
2 tablespoons butter
6 ounces wild
   mushrooms (such as
   chanterelles or
   shiitakes), sliced
3 tablespoons dry white
   wine
Salt and freshly ground
   black pepper to taste

There's something very satisfying about a hearty steak sandwich, and we think you'll enjoy this recipe. The shallots give a more subtle flavor than onions, which are typical accompaniments to steak sandwiches, and the mushrooms complement both the flavor and texture of the beef. Lightly pounding the steaks helps tenderize them, and also makes them easier to eat.

Prepare the potatoes.

To prepare the mushrooms and shallots, heat the olive oil in a nonstick saucepan and sauté the shallots over medium heat for 6 or 7 minutes, until lightly browned. Add the butter and the mushrooms and sauté for 5 or 6 minutes longer, until soft. Turn down the heat, add the wine, and reduce until the mixture is thick and moist and most of the liquid has evaporated, about 4 to 5 minutes. Season with salt and pepper and keep warm.

Lightly pound the steaks 2 or 3 times with a meat mallet or rolling pin and season with salt, pepper, and Worcestershire sauce. Heat the olive oil in a skillet set over medium-high heat and sear the steaks for about 1½ minutes on each side. Turn down the heat to medium and sauté for 1 minute longer for medium-rare, 1½ to 2 minutes for medium, or to the desired doneness.

To serve, spread each side of the rolls with mustard. Place the steak on the bottom half and top with the warm mushrooms and shallots. Serve open-faced.

WINE SUGGESTION: *A West Coast Pinot Noir or a regional French Burgundy should transform this sandwich platter into a banquet.*

The best bets for finding multi-grain rolls or bread (also called "7-grain" or "4-grain") are health food stores or good-quality bakeries. Sometimes multi-grain bread is labeled "health bread."

FOR THE SANDWICHES:

4 top sirloin steaks, prime or choice grade, about 6 ounces each and ½ inch thick

Salt and freshly ground black pepper to taste

2 teaspoons Worcestershire sauce

1 tablespoon olive oil

4 multi-grain rolls, sliced in half crosswise (or 8 slices multi-grain bread), toasted

¼ cup Dijon mustard, or to taste

ORANGE-JALAPEÑO BEEF BACK RIBS WITH CHEDDAR-POBLANO CORN BREAD

Serves 4

**FOR THE BEEF RIBS
AND ORANGE-
JALAPEÑO MARINADE:**

4 pounds beef back ribs,
   choice grade or better,
   cut about 6 inches
   wide

2 teaspoons olive oil

3 jalapeño chiles, minced

3 shallots, minced

3 garlic cloves, minced

1½ cups freshly squeezed
   orange juice

1 cup apple cider vinegar

¼ cup dark molasses

The orange-jalapeño marinade works well with beef back ribs, beef short ribs, pork ribs, and even chicken. The ribs should be marinated overnight and can be braised in advance and then refrigerated until ready to grill. Braising the ribs in the marinade enhances the flavor and speeds up the grilling time, but is not absolutely necessary. If you choose not to braise the ribs first, grill the ribs on a rack over low heat in a covered barbecue for at least 3 hours. The corn bread is very rich, dense, and wonderful, and definitely does not need any additional butter for spreading.

Place the ribs in a deep baking pan large enough to accommodate them. Heat the olive oil in a skillet and sauté the jalapeños and shallots over medium heat for about 3 or 4 minutes. Add the remaining marinade ingredients, bring to a simmer, and pour over the ribs. Let cool and marinate for 1 or 2 days in the refrigerator, turning once or twice if they are not fully immersed. Bring to room temperature before braising.

Preheat the oven to 300 degrees. Place the baking pan with the ribs and marinade in the oven and braise, covered, for about 1 hour or until the meat is beginning to get tender, but not falling off the bone.

Prepare the grill. Turn up the oven temperature to 375 degrees.

Drain the marinade into a saucepan and reduce over medium heat until slightly thickened, about 10 minutes. Skim any fat from the surface with a spoon. Grill the ribs, covered, about 30 minutes. Remove the cover and continue to grill for 30 minutes, or until very tender, glazing occasionally with the marinade. Slice each rack of ribs into manageable-sized pieces, or individual rib bones. Serve any remaining glaze on the side.

While the ribs are grilling, prepare the corn bread. In a mixing bowl, combine the baking powder with the cornmeal. Add the eggs, sour cream, creamed corn, butter, cheese, and poblano. Heat the vegetable oil in a cast-iron skillet and wipe it around all sides to coat. When the skillet is hot, pour in the batter, and bake for 30 to 35 minutes, or until golden brown.

Serve the ribs with the corn bread and garnish with the chiles and parsley.

WINE SUGGESTION: *A French Côtes-du-Rhône or a West Coast Pinot Noir will blend effectively with the complex and robust nuances of this dish.*

FOR THE CHEDDAR-POBLANO CORN BREAD:

1 tablespoon baking powder

1 cup cornmeal, preferably stone-ground

2 eggs, lightly beaten

1 cup sour cream

1 cup canned creamed corn

¼ cup melted butter

1 cup grated Cheddar cheese

1 poblano chile, roasted, peeled, seeded, and diced (page 208)

2 tablespoons vegetable oil

4 red serrano or jalapeño chiles, for garnish (optional)

4 sprigs parsley, for garnish (optional)

The corn bread recipe is virtually foolproof. It can even be mixed ahead and baked when needed. (We have actually mixed the batter to take camping and then cooked it in an iron skillet over the fire.) Stone-ground cornmeal provides more texture, but any kind works fine. You may bake the corn bread in a 9-inch square baking pan, if you prefer.

THAI BEEF SALAD IN A BEEFSTEAK TOMATO

Serves 4 as a main course, or 8 as an appetizer

FOR THE LIME-CILANTRO DRESSING:

⅔ cup freshly squeezed lime juice (from 3 or 4 limes)

¼ cup Asian fish sauce, such as nam pla

1 or 2 jalapeño chiles (to taste), roughly chopped

3 garlic cloves, smashed

1 cup roughly chopped cilantro, including stems

FOR THE GARNISH:

½ cup uncooked jasmine rice (or other type of fragrant rice such as basmati)

½ cup unsalted raw peanuts, chopped

¼ cup cilantro leaves

This recipe makes a wonderful summer main course, but you can also use smaller tomatoes and serve it as an appetizer. For large gatherings, use it as an accompaniment; for example, with the Orange-Jalapeño Beef Back Ribs (page 62). The recipe can be prepared a day in advance and stuffed into the tomatoes just before serving. It is best when served slightly chilled or at room temperature. Other attractive garnishes to consider for the salad are sliced radishes, cucumbers, or red onions. Substitute minced leftover steak for the ground beef if you wish.

To prepare the dressing, put the lime juice, fish sauce, chiles, garlic, and cilantro in a blender and puree. Before serving, taste the dressing and add more minced jalapeño if desired.

Preheat the oven to 350 degrees.

To prepare the garnish, heat the rice in a nonstick pan over high heat and toast, swirling and shaking the pan for about 10 minutes or until the rice is fragrant and brown (be careful not to scorch the rice, but it should be well toasted). Set aside, let cool, and grind to a powder in a spice grinder. In the same pan, toast the peanuts over medium-high heat for about 5 minutes, or until golden brown; take care not to burn. Let cool and chop.

To prepare the salad, cut the eggplant in half lengthwise and lightly oil the cut side with the 1 teaspoon of olive oil. Roast the eggplant cut side down on a baking

FOR THE BEEF SALAD:

1 eggplant (about 1
  pound)
1 tablespoon plus 1
  teaspoon olive oil
5 garlic cloves, chopped
2 shallots, thinly sliced
8 ounces lean high-
  quality coarsely
  ground beef or
  coarsely ground chuck
  steak
8 ounces spinach, well
  rinsed, stems removed
4 scallions (green with
  some white parts),
  thinly sliced
2 cups cooked Jasmine
  Rice, cooled (page 203)
½ cup Lime-Cilantro
  Dressing (see opposite
  page)
1 pound mesclun salad
  mix

4 beefsteak tomatoes or 4
  red Roma tomatoes
  and 4 yellow Roma
  tomatoes, tops
  removed and insides
  scooped out

sheet in the oven for about 1 hour, or until tender. When
cool enough, remove the pulp with a spoon and chop.

Heat the 1 tablespoon of olive oil in a large heavy skillet over high heat, add the garlic, and stir rapidly for 2 or
3 minutes, until it just begins to brown. Turn down the
heat to medium-high, stir in the shallots, and sauté for 3
minutes longer. Add the beef and cook for about 5 minutes or until just browned, using a fork to break up any
lumps. Remove from the heat and drain off any fat. Add
the spinach to the pan and cover briefly to allow the
spinach to wilt, about 3 minutes. Transfer the mixture to

a mixing bowl and let cool. Add the scallions, chopped eggplant, and cooked rice and stir to incorporate. Add ½ cup of the dressing to the ground beef mixture and stir gently to combine.

Toss the mesclun salad mix with enough of the remaining dressing to lightly coat; serve the rest of the dressing at the table. Place the mesclun salad on chilled plates. Make 5 partial cuts down the sides of the tomatoes so that they open like the petals of a flower. Lay the tomatoes in the center of the greens on each plate and mound an equal portion of the beef salad in each tomato. Sprinkle the rice powder and peanuts and garnish with cilantro leaves.

WINE SUGGESTION: *Although wine is rarely selected to accompany a salad dish, in this case a light acidic red wine such as a Spanish Rioja would be pleasingly harmonious. Alternatively, serve a fruity white wine such as Gewürztraminer from Alsace or California.*

The roasted rice powder is delicious on salads and soups and will keep for several weeks in a tightly covered container in the refrigerator or in a cool dark place; the same is true for the toasted chopped peanuts. It is important to purchase the jasmine rice in a store with high turnover, otherwise it may have sat on the shelf for a long time and have lost its aromatic quality. Don't bother to make the rice powder unless it is top quality. For the cooked rice used to stuff the tomatoes, by all means use leftover rice.

If Asian fish sauce is unavailable, you may substitute 3 tablespoons soy sauce mixed with 4 smashed anchovies.

TEQUILA-MARINATED GRILLED STEAK FAJITAS WITH JALAPEÑO BEANS AND GRILLED VEGETABLES

Serves 4

Fajitas (literally "belts" in Spanish) are one of the most popular Southwestern dishes, and they actually originated in Texas at the end of the last century. Fajitas can be made with chicken and seafood as well as beef, and in this recipe, the tequila and citrus marinade gives the steak a robust tang. After the vegetables have been grilled, you may serve them as they are or cut them into smaller, bite-sized pieces. If you have a grill basket, you can cut the vegetables into smaller portions before marinating and grilling, or alternatively, thread the vegetables on skewers to keep them from slipping through the grate of the grill.

....

To prepare the marinade, combine the citrus juices and zests, tequila, vinegar, 1 tablespoon of the olive oil, the garlic, and red pepper flakes in a mixing bowl. Divide the marinade in half, transferring each half to a large shallow bowl or glass dish. Add the steak to one half, cover, and marinate for 2 to 3 hours in the refrigerator, turning the steaks occasionally. Remove the steaks from the refrigerator and let them sit at room temperature for 1 hour before grilling.

To the other half of the marinade, add the remaining ⅓ cup of the olive oil.

Add the onions, tomatoes, bell peppers, and zucchini, and gently toss to coat. Let marinate for at least 1 hour, tossing occasionally. About 15 minutes before grilling, add the mushrooms to the marinade.

FOR THE TEQUILA MARINADE:
Juice and zest of 6 limes

Juice and zest of 4 oranges

½ cup tequila (preferably Herradura Silver or Sauza Hornitos)

½ cup unseasoned rice vinegar

⅓ cup plus 1 tablespoon olive oil

4 garlic cloves, minced

2 teaspoons dried red pepper flakes

FOR THE BEEF:
3 top sirloin steaks, prime or choice grade, about 8 ounces each and 1 inch to 1¼ inches thick

For the Vegetables:

3 large onions, cut
   crosswise into 3 or 4
   slices
6 Roma tomatoes, cut in
   half lengthwise
2 red bell peppers,
   seeded and halved
2 zucchini, sliced
   lengthwise into 4
   strips
6 ounces cultivated
   mushrooms

For the Jalapeño Beans:

1 tablespoon olive oil
1 cup finely diced onion
¼ cup finely diced red
   bell pepper
2 jalapeño chiles, seeded
   and minced
1 can pinto beans (15
   ounces), drained
1 can black beans (15
   ounces), drained
1 cup chicken stock or
   water
¼ teaspoon salt
½ tablespoon minced
   marjoram

Prepare the grill.

About 40 minutes before you are ready to serve, drain the marinated vegetables and reserve the marinade. Thread the mushrooms (and tomatoes, if desired) on skewers. Grill the vegetables until they become tender and begin to blacken, 15 to 20 minutes; brush them with some of the marinade as they grill. Remove and slice the bell pepper and zucchini into strips and cut the onions in half. Remove the mushrooms and tomatoes from the skewers and slice the mushrooms and tomatoes in half lengthwise. Set aside and keep warm.

To prepare the beans, heat the olive oil in a large pan and sauté the onion, bell pepper, and jalapeños over medium heat for 4 or 5 minutes, until softened. Stir in the beans, add the stock, and cook for 10 minutes or until the liquid is somewhat reduced and thicker. Season with salt and add the marjoram.

About 15 minutes before serving, remove the meat from the marinade. Grill the steaks for about 4 minutes on each side for medium-rare, 5 minutes for medium, or to the desired doneness, depending on how thick the cut is and how hot the grill is. Remove the steaks from the grill and slice across the grain.

Just before serving, heat the flour tortillas on the grill, about 30 seconds on each side, until warm but not browned. (Alternatively, warm them in a dry skillet on the stove top.)

To serve, arrange the sliced steak and vegetables on a warm platter or in a heated iron skillet. Arrange the tortillas in a covered basket or wrapped in a cloth. Serve the salsa, beans, sour cream, and cheese in festive bowls on the side. Guests should serve themselves by filling a warm tortilla with a mix of steak and vegetables of their choosing, topped with salsa, sour cream, and grated cheese.

Wine Suggestion: *A California Pinot Noir or Spanish Rioja.*

If grilling is not an option, fajitas can be easily prepared on the stovetop; simply marinate the steak and vegetables in the same way and then sauté the steak and vegetables separately in a small amount of peanut oil, or roast the vegetables in the oven.

In this recipe we use sirloin rather than the traditional skirt steak, which is a less tender cut; leaner cuts are typically used for especially tender, tasty fajitas. We suggest 1½ pounds of steaks, but for heartier appetites, or leftovers, you may wish to use 2 pounds.

FOR SERVING:

8 flour tortillas

1 recipe Salsa Fresca (page 45)

½ cup sour cream (optional)

1 cup grated Monterey Jack or Cheddar cheese (optional)

TENDERLOIN TIPS IN PITA POCKETS WITH YOGURT-TAHINI DRESSING

Serves 4

FOR THE YOGURT-TAHINI DRESSING:

1 cup plain whole-milk yogurt

2 tablespoons tahini

2 tablespoons freshly squeezed lemon juice

1 tablespoon chopped parsley

¼ teaspoon salt

Here's a recipe that has a definite Middle Eastern influence. Tahini is a paste made from sesame seeds that is common in the cuisine of the region; pita flat bread and yogurt are also ingredients typical of many Middle Eastern countries. It's important to use the kind of pita bread that can be slit open and filled; some types—including those available at Middle Eastern markets—do not open. This recipe is quick to prepare once you have made the dry rub; the beef does not need to be marinated, and the tenderloin tips cook in minutes. Sauté the meat just before serving as the tenderloin tips will toughen if cooked in advance and reheated later. Serve with Couscous Salad (page 94), if you wish.

To prepare the dressing, place the yogurt, tahini, lemon juice, parsley, and salt in a small mixing bowl and combine thoroughly. Keep refrigerated.

To prepare the dry rub, grind the coriander and cumin seeds with the cinnamon stick in a coffee grinder or mortar and pestle. Transfer to a mixing bowl and combine with the chile powder, paprika, peppercorns, and salt.

To prepare the tenderloin tips, toss with the dry rub mixture to cover all sides. Heat the olive oil in a large skillet and sauté the meat over medium-high heat, turning the meat so that all sides get browned and cooked to the desired doneness, about 2 or 3 minutes for medium-rare and 3 to 4 minutes for medium. You may need to sauté the meat in batches so as not to overcrowd the pan.

To serve, cut off the end of each pita bread and open to form a pocket. In a mixing bowl, combine the lettuce, tomatoes, and onion with enough dressing to lightly coat the salad. Place a small amount of the salad in the bottom of each pita and fill with the sautéed tenderloin tips. Drizzle some of the Yogurt-Tahini Dressing over the meat, and top with another spoonful of salad.

WINE SUGGESTION: *A West Coast Pinot Noir, or a regional French Burgundy.*

If you cannot find it at your local store, plain whole-milk yogurt should be available at any health food store. Likewise the tahini, which is also available at Middle Eastern stores. To use low-fat yogurt in place of whole-milk yogurt, drain 1¼ cups low-fat yogurt through cheesecloth or a coffee filter for about 1 hour before you mix the dressing. If you prefer a thicker, richer sauce, replace up to half of the yogurt with sour cream.

FOR THE DRY RUB:

2 teaspoons coriander seeds, toasted (page 209)

2 teaspoons cumin seeds, toasted (page 209)

1 (2-inch) length of cinnamon stick, broken into pieces, toasted (page 209)

1 tablespoon mild red chile powder

2 tablespoons hot paprika

1 tablespoon black peppercorns, crushed

1 teaspoon salt

FOR THE TENDERLOIN TIPS:

1 pound tenderloin tips, choice grade, cut into large dice

1 tablespoon olive oil

FOR SERVING:

4 pita breads

5 or 6 large romaine lettuce leaves, julienned

2 tomatoes, diced

¼ onion, diced

CHRIS SCHLESINGER'S GRILLED LIME-MARINATED FLANK STEAK WITH CHIPOTLE-HONEY SAUCE

Serves 4

For the Beef and Marinade:

2½ pounds flank steak, choice grade

1 canned chipotle chile, chopped

2 garlic cloves, chopped

1 tablespoon chopped cilantro

¼ cup vegetable oil

10 tablespoons freshly squeezed lime juice (about 5 limes)

Salt and freshly ground black pepper to taste

Chris Schlesinger is the owner of the acclaimed East Coast Grill in Cambridge, Massachusetts, and the author of several cookbooks, most notably on the fine art of grilling and on salsas. His Inner Beauty line of hot sauces and spice rubs is popular with heat aficionados. In this mouthwatering recipe, Chris uses the less tender flank steak because he finds it so flavorful, and he tenderizes it by using a marinade.

Place the steak in a large dish or baking pan. Mix together the chipotle, garlic, cilantro, vegetable oil, and lime juice in a bowl and pour over the steak. Cover, and marinate in the refrigerator for 4 to 6 hours, turning occasionally.

Prepare the grill.

To prepare the sauce, combine the chipotles, honey, peanut oil, vinegar, mustard, lime juice, garlic, and cumin in a blender or food processor and puree until smooth. Stir in the cilantro and season with salt and pepper.

Remove the steak and season with salt and pepper. Grill over high heat for about 5 minutes on each side for medium-rare, 7 minutes on each side for medium, or to the desired doneness. Remove the steak from the grill and let it rest for 4 or 5 minutes. With a sharp knife, thinly slice the steak across the grain and at a sharp angle.

Serve the steak on top of a slice of the French bread and accompany each serving with several tablespoons of the sauce.

WINE SUGGESTION: *Try a Spanish red wine such as Rioja or a Gamay Beaujolais from California.*

The acid from the lime juice and vinegar in the sauce complements the charred flavor of the meat very well; however, take care not to marinate the steak for longer than 4 to 6 hours as the acid will "cook" the steak, causing it to turn gray in color. For notes on canned chipotle chiles, see page xii.

FOR THE CHIPOTLE-HONEY SAUCE:

3 canned chipotle chiles, pureed

$\frac{1}{4}$ cup honey

2 tablespoons peanut oil

2 tablespoons balsamic vinegar

2 tablespoons brown mustard

$\frac{1}{2}$ cup freshly squeezed lime juice (about 4 limes)

2 garlic cloves

1 teaspoon ground cumin

2 tablespoons chopped cilantro

1 teaspoon salt

Freshly cracked black pepper, to taste

4 slices crusty French bread, cut at an angle

SUMMER BURGERS WITH ALAN'S ASIAN GUACAMOLE

Serves 4

For Alan's Asian Guacamole:

2 ripe avocados, peeled, pitted, and diced

½ cup diced onion

½ cup diced tomato

3 tablespoons sake

¼ cup sliced scallions (green part only)

2 tablespoons freshly squeezed lime juice

2 tablespoons minced fresh ginger

1 tablespoon chopped cilantro

1 tablespoon vegetable oil

½ teaspoon chile sauce with garlic (such as Sambal Oelek)

1 teaspoon Alan's Chile Pepper Water (see sidebar, page 75), or ¼ teaspoon finely minced jalapeño chile

1 teaspoon salt or to taste

This recipe combines beef burgers tweaked with Pacific Rim flavors and a refreshingly different guacamole from one of Hawaii's premier chefs, Alan Wong. Alan and his restaurant, Alan Wong's, are major reasons why Honolulu is now a travel destination for food lovers. Although you won't find burgers on Alan's menu, his Asian Guacamole pairs wonderfully well with grilled fish and poultry. You may also wish to serve it with a bowl of tortilla chips at your next party.

....

Combine all the guacamole ingredients in a mixing bowl and mix gently without mashing the avocado. Serve immediately or cover and refrigerate.

Prepare the grill.

To prepare the burgers, heat the sesame oil in a small saucepan over medium heat. Add the onions and sauté for about 5 minutes, until softened. Add the ginger, garlic, and red and green peppers and continue to sauté for 2 or 3 minutes. Remove from the heat, transfer to a large bowl, and cool. Add the beef, scallions, and cilantro, and gently mix to combine. Add the soy sauce gradually, adding just enough to flavor the beef but not so much that the mixture becomes soggy so that the burgers will not hold together. Set aside in the refrigerator.

Divide the beef mixture into 4 equal pieces, form with your hands into balls, and then flatten to make patties. Heat the vegetable oil in a large nonstick sauté pan. Sear the burgers over medium-high heat for 1 minute on each side. Turn down the heat to medium and continue to cook for about 3 minutes per side, or until the internal temperature reaches 160 degrees. Split the rolls in half and toast until golden brown; serve the burgers open-faced on the rolls. Top with a generous helping of guacamole, or serve it on the side. Serve with the Shoestring Potatoes.

WINE SUGGESTION: *A lighter-style California Merlot or a St. Émilion from France would work best.*

Alan's Chile Pepper Water, used in the guacamole, is a mild all-purpose table condiment popular in Hawaii. To make it, combine in a blender ⅓ cup cold water, 1 garlic clove, 1 red serrano chile (or ½ jalapeño), 1 tablespoon white vinegar, 2 teaspoons minced ginger, and a pinch of salt. Puree until smooth. Bring 1¼ cups of water to a boil in a saucepan, add the puree, return to a boil, then remove from the heat and let cool. Transfer to a glass bottle and keep refrigerated. Use as a seasoning for salads or fish dishes, or place it on your table during mealtimes and use it as a condiment. This will keep 2 to 3 weeks if refrigerated.

FOR THE BURGERS:

3 tablespoons toasted sesame oil
2 onions, finely diced
3 tablespoons minced ginger
4 garlic cloves, minced
½ red bell pepper, seeded and diced
½ green bell pepper, seeded and diced
1¼ pounds high-quality lean ground beef
3 scallions, finely sliced
2 tablespoons chopped cilantro
¼ cup Tabasco Soy Sauce (or ¼ cup soy sauce mixed with ½ teaspoon Tabasco sauce)

1 tablespoon vegetable oil
4 large sesame-seed rolls or hamburger buns, toasted
1 recipe Shoestring Potatoes (page 17)

GRILLED PORTERHOUSE STEAKS WITH TOMATO CHARLOTTE

Serves 4

FOR THE BASIL BUTTER:

2 tablespoons butter, at room temperature

$\frac{1}{4}$ teaspoon finely minced garlic

$\frac{1}{2}$ teaspoon freshly squeezed lemon juice

$\frac{1}{2}$ tablespoon minced basil

Salt and freshly ground black pepper to taste

This simple dish is sure to delight any steak lover and is not for the faint of heart! Tomatoes form a natural partnership with beef. If you use vine-ripened, good-quality tomatoes for this recipe, you will be rewarded with a very intense and flavorful side dish, a savory variation on the classic "charlotte" dessert. In addition, the basil really brings out the full flavor of the tomatoes.

Preheat the oven to 350 degrees. If using charcoal, preheat the grill 30 minutes before cooking the steaks; otherwise, preheat a gas grill shortly before using.

To prepare the butter, thoroughly mix together the butter, garlic, lemon juice, and basil in a small bowl. Season with salt and pepper. Place in a small ramekin or tub and form into a smooth butter pat. Chill in the refrigerator. Just before serving, cut into 4 pieces.

To prepare the charlotte, butter an 8 by 6-inch baking dish and place 2 layers of the tomatoes in the bottom. Sprinkle with 1 teaspoon of the sugar and half of the basil. Season with salt and pepper and cover with half of the bread crumbs. Dot with half of the sliced butter. Repeat with the remaining tomatoes, sugar, and basil, and season with salt and pepper. Top with the remaining bread crumbs and butter. Bake in the oven for 30 minutes, or until the bread crumb topping is golden and crisp.

Season the steaks with salt and pepper, and grill for 3 to 4 minutes per side for medium-rare, 4 to 5 minutes

FOR THE TOMATO
CHARLOTTE:

FOR THE TOMATO
CHARLOTTE:

2 pounds tomatoes,
blanched (page 207),
peeled, and diced
2 teaspoons superfine
sugar
2 tablespoons chopped
basil
Salt and freshly ground
black pepper to taste
2 cups coarse fresh bread
crumbs
2 tablespoons chilled
butter, thinly sliced

FOR THE STEAKS:
4 porterhouse steaks,
prime or choice grade,
about 16 ounces each
¼ teaspoon salt
¼ teaspoon freshly
ground black pepper

4 sprigs Italian flat-leaf
parsley or basil, for
garnish

for medium, or to desired doneness. Transfer to warm
serving plates and immediately place about ½ teaspoon
of the butter on each steak. Serve with the charlotte and
garnish with the parsley.

WINE SUGGESTION: *A big steak deserves a big wine, such as
a Cabernet Sauvignon from California, a red Bordeaux
from France, or one of the great Italian reds from Tuscany.*

You can add the charlotte to angel-hair pasta lightly dressed with
pesto sauce for a wonderful, summery lunch dish.

For the Moussaka:

2 large eggplants, about
1¾ pounds total

Salt to taste

6 tablespoons olive oil

2 large onions, diced

1½ pounds lean high-
quality ground beef

2 tomatoes (8 ounces),
diced

2 tablespoons tomato
paste

½ cup red wine

½ teaspoon ground
cinnamon

1 teaspoon dried mixed
herbs (such as Herbes
de Provence)

Freshly ground black
pepper to taste

Moussaka is a popular casserole-style dish in Greece, Turkey, and many other Middle Eastern countries. Typically, moussaka contains ground beef or lamb, eggplant (the round, purple type), and a cheese sauce, but some versions contain just eggplant and other vegetables, or potatoes and beef. Of the many versions we tried, this is the best!

To prepare the moussaka, cut the eggplants crosswise into thin slices and place on a large platter. Sprinkle with salt, cover with plastic wrap, and let sit for 30 minutes. Rinse the slices and drain.

Heat 2 tablespoons of the olive oil in a large saucepan, add the onions, and sauté over medium-high heat until lightly golden brown, about 7 or 8 minutes. Add the ground beef, tomatoes, tomato paste, red wine, cinnamon, herbs, and season with salt and pepper. Stirring occasionally, cook until all of the beef is browned, about 10 to 12 minutes longer.

Heat 2 tablespoons of the remaining olive oil in a large sauté pan and add one-third of the eggplant slices in a single layer. Sauté over medium-high heat for 3 to 4 minutes on each side until just tender and lightly browned. Remove with a slotted spoon and drain on paper towels. Add 1 tablespoon more of the olive oil and when hot, add another one-third of the eggplant slices, repeating the cooking process; remove and drain. Add the remaining 1 tablespoon of oil and the remaining eggplant slices and repeat. Set aside.

To prepare the sauce, heat the milk in a saucepan, add the onion and garlic, and bring just to a boil. Turn off the heat and let sit for 30 minutes to infuse. Strain, reserving the milk. Meanwhile, preheat the oven to 350 degrees.

Heat the butter in a saucepan and when melted, add the flour, stirring constantly over low heat for 2 minutes. Gradually add the infused milk and when completely blended in, bring to a boil over medium heat while stirring. When the sauce thickens, remove from the heat and stir in the mustard and cheese. Whisk in the eggs, and season with the nutmeg and salt and pepper to taste.

Line a large lightly oiled casserole or ovenproof baking dish with one-third of the cooked eggplant and arrange an even layer of one-third of the beef mixture on top. Cover with one-third of the sauce. Arrange another layer of each, and then a third and final layer, ending with the sauce.

To prepare the topping, if using, heat the butter over medium heat in a sauté pan and when melted, add the bread crumbs. Stir together over medium heat until thoroughly combined. Remove from the heat and sprinkle evenly over the top of the moussaka. Cover the casserole (use foil if necessary, but make sure it is not touching the topping) and place in the oven. Bake for 45 minutes. Remove the cover and cook for 15 to 20 minutes longer, or until the topping is a dark golden brown; take care that it does not burn. Remove from the oven, let cool for 5 minutes, and serve.

WINE SUGGESTION: *A West Coast Merlot/Cabernet blend or a regional St. Émilion from France are soft enough to "marry" successfully with this dish.*

FOR THE CHEESE SAUCE:

2 cups milk
½ onion, chopped
2 garlic cloves, chopped
½ cup butter
¼ cup all-purpose flour
1 teaspoon Dijon
   mustard
1 cup grated Cheddar
   cheese (4 ounces)
2 eggs, lightly beaten
¼ teaspoon ground
   nutmeg, or to taste
Salt and pepper to taste

FOR THE TOPPING (OPTIONAL):

2 tablespoons butter
½ cup prepared fine
   bread crumbs

Salting the eggplant slices and letting them sit causes them to "sweat" and lose their bitterness; younger, less mature eggplants tend to have less natural bitterness, but it's still a good idea to salt them. Serve the moussaka with a green salad, if desired.

SKEWERED BEEF SATAY WITH SPICY PEANUT SAUCE AND BELL PEPPER CHUTNEY

Serves 4 as a main course, or 8 as an appetizer

For the Marinade:

3 tablespoons peanut oil

½ onion, diced

¼ teaspoon minced fresh ginger

2 tablespoons coconut milk

1 tablespoon freshly squeezed lime juice

1 teaspoon dark molasses

½ teaspoon chile sauce with garlic (such as Sambal Oelek)

½ teaspoon ground coriander

½ teaspoon ground cumin

½ teaspoon salt

For the Beef:

2 boneless rib-eye steaks, prime or choice grade, 8 ounces each, trimmed of all fat

16 bamboo skewers, soaked in water for at least 30 minutes and drained

Satay is a Southeast Asian dish that can be made with almost any meat. Call us biased, but the robust flavor of beef sets off the delicious sweet-and-spicy sauce the best. The satay style originated in Indonesia (probably by way of India from the Middle East), but similar versions are popular in other countries such as Malaysia and Thailand. The peanut sauce is highly versatile, and we also use it for the Thai Meatballs (page 127).

To prepare the marinade, heat the oil in a sauté pan, add the onion, and sauté over medium-high heat for 5 minutes. Add the ginger and cook for 2 minutes longer. Transfer to a shallow dish and add the remaining marinade ingredients.

Cut the steaks across into 3-inch lengths and then cut ⅛-inch strips. Place the beef strips in the marinade, covering with the liquid, and marinate for 30 minutes at room temperature or up to 2 hours in the refrigerator.

When ready to broil, remove the beef from the marinade and thread 2 or 3 of the steak strips lengthwise onto each skewer. Leave at least 1 inch of skewer uncovered at the blunt end for easy handling.

To prepare the chutney, heat the peanut oil in a sauté pan. Add the onion, garlic, ginger, bell peppers, and chile, and sauté over medium-high heat for 6 or 7 minutes until soft, stirring often. Lower the heat to medium-low, add the honey, citrus juices, fish sauce, and chile paste. Season with salt to taste and sauté for 10 minutes longer or until completely soft and little liquid remains. Transfer to a serving bowl and let cool.

Preheat the broiler (or prepare the grill). Broil (or grill) the skewered beef for 2 to 3 minutes on the first side and for 2 minutes on the other side for medium, or to the desired doneness. Serve 4 skewers per plate with the rice and chutney. Ladle some of the sauce over the meat on each plate and serve the rest in a bowl on the side.

WINE SUGGESTION: *A hearty Cabernet from anywhere in the world will complement this dish nicely.*

The beef should be cut thinly, and to make this easier, place it in the freezer for 20 to 30 minutes ahead of time; the firmer texture facilitates cutting neatly with the grain.

FOR THE BELL PEPPER CHUTNEY:

1 tablespoon peanut oil
1 onion, diced
3 garlic cloves, minced
1 teaspoon minced ginger
1 green bell pepper, seeded and diced
1 red bell pepper, seeded and diced
1 green or red Thai chile (or 2 serrano chiles), minced (with seeds)
1 tablespoon honey
1 tablespoon freshly squeezed lime juice
2 tablespoons freshly squeezed lemon juice
2 teaspoons Asian fish sauce, such as nam pla
½ teaspoon chile paste with garlic (such as Sambal Oelek)
Salt to taste
1 recipe Spicy Peanut Sauce (page 127)
1 recipe Short-Grain Sticky Rice (page 204)

GRILLED STRIP STEAKS WITH PROVENÇALE RATATOUILLE AND POTATOES ANNA PINWHEELS

Serves 4

FOR THE RATATOUILLE:

3 tablespoons extra-
   virgin olive oil
½ cup diced onion
½ cup seeded and diced
   red bell pepper
2 Roma tomatoes,
   blanched, peeled,
   seeded, and diced
   (page 207)
1 teaspoon finely minced
   garlic
½ teaspoon minced
   thyme
Salt and freshly ground
   black pepper to taste
½ cup diced zucchini
   (unpeeled)
½ cup diced eggplant
   (unpeeled)
6 basil leaves, thinly
   sliced

This ratatouille recipe brings the bright, clear, and summery flavors of the Provence region of France to your dining table. The crisp texture of the potatoes contrasts with the smooth yet chunky ratatouille and the rich, soft steak.

Preheat the oven to 350 degrees. Prepare the grill.

To prepare the ratatouille, heat 1½ tablespoons of the olive oil in a heavy saucepan and cook the onion over low heat for 3 or 4 minutes, until soft and translucent. Add the bell pepper and cook for another 3 minutes. Stir in the tomatoes, garlic, thyme, and a pinch of salt and pepper. Continue cooking for 8 minutes, being careful not to overcook. Remove from the heat and set aside. Heat another ½ tablespoon of the olive oil in a sauté pan and sauté the zucchini over medium heat for 3 or 4 minutes, or until lightly colored. Season with salt and pepper, add to the tomato mixture, and set aside. Using the same pan that was used for the zucchini, heat the remaining 1 tablespoon of olive oil and sauté the eggplant over medium heat for 5 minutes, or until soft. Season with salt and pepper and transfer to a colander to drain. Add the eggplant to the saucepan with the zucchini and tomato mixture and sprinkle with the basil. Cook over medium heat for 3 or 4 minutes, stirring gently. Adjust the seasonings if necessary and let cool.

To prepare the potatoes, lightly butter parchment paper set on a baking sheet. Cut the potatoes crosswise into very thin slices, pat dry, and arrange in a single layer on the parchment paper in 8 small circular pinwheel patterns with the slices overlapping. Brush the pinwheels with the butter and sprinkle with salt and pepper. Bake in the oven for 20 to 25 minutes or until golden and crisp.

While the potatoes are cooking, season the steaks with salt and pepper and grill over medium-high heat for about 4 to 4½ minutes on each side for medium-rare, about 5 minutes for medium, or to the desired doneness. Serve each steak with 2 potato pinwheels (overlapping each other) and the ratatouille.

WINE SUGGESTION: *A fine Cabernet Sauvignon from Bordeaux or California.*

FOR THE POTATOES:

3 russet potatoes, about 8 ounces each, peeled
2 tablespoons butter, melted
Salt and freshly ground black pepper to taste

FOR THE STEAKS:

4 boneless strip steaks, prime or choice grade, about 10 ounces each and 1 inch thick
Salt and freshly ground black pepper to taste

Instead of grilling, the steaks can be pan-seared in a hot cast-iron skillet set over medium-high heat; the cooking time will be about the same.

SKEWERED SURF AND TURF WITH RICE AND ROASTED GARLIC SAUCE

Serves 4

FOR THE ROASTED GARLIC SAUCE:

2 heads garlic

2 tablespoons olive oil

1 small onion, diced

1½ cups chicken stock

1 cup heavy cream

2 teaspoons minced
   marjoram

¼ teaspoon salt

¼ teaspoon freshly
   ground black pepper

The combination of surf and turf is a classic and remains popular, even if some people consider it an old-fashioned cliché (these are the people missing out on one of life's great culinary pleasures!). Summertime brings a new crop of garlic in the stores, and the purple-tinged variety is our favorite for this recipe because of its sweeter flavor. If you like garlic, you'll love this sauce, which can also be used alone with pasta or ravioli.

Preheat the oven to 350 degrees.

To prepare the garlic sauce, break up the heads of garlic into individual cloves, keeping them unpeeled. Place in a roasting pan and roast in the oven for about 30 minutes, or until lightly browned, shaking the pan occasionally. Remove from the oven, and when cool enough, squeeze out the garlic from the cloves and mince. Place the olive oil in a saucepan and sauté the onion over medium-high heat for 3 minutes. Add the garlic and sauté for 2 minutes longer. Add the stock and cream and bring to a boil. Turn down the heat and simmer for 10 minutes. Add the marjoram, salt, and pepper and remove from the heat. Transfer to a blender and puree. Return to a clean saucepan and simmer, uncovered, for about 30 minutes or until the sauce is reduced by one-third. Just before serving, warm through in a saucepan.

Prepare the grill.

For the Surf and Turf:

¼ cup (2 ounces) melted butter

1 teaspoon freshly squeezed lemon juice

2 frozen cold-water rock lobster tails (about 6 ounces each)

½ teaspoon paprika

1 pound tenderloin tips, prime or choice grade, or top sirloin cut into ¾-inch cubes

8 scallops (or 4 jumbo scallops)

4 long metal skewers or 8 bamboo skewers, soaked in water for at least 30 minutes and drained

1 recipe Long-Grain White Rice (page 205)

8 thin lemon slices, for garnish

4 sprigs dill, for garnish

To prepare the surf and turf, mix the butter and lemon juice in a mixing bowl.

With scissors, cut the two lobster shells to expose the meat, brush with the butter mixture, and grill over medium-high heat, shell side down, for 5 minutes. Turn over, brushing any exposed lobster meat with the butter mixture, and grill for 7 minutes longer, or until the meat is white and cooked through. Add the paprika to the remaining butter mixture and when the lobster is cool enough, remove each shell, brush the tails with the paprika butter, and cut each tail into 6 slices.

Thread the tenderloin tips and scallops on the skewers, brushing the scallops with the butter mixture, and grill for 3 to 4 minutes on each side, or to the desired doneness, basting the scallops.

Serve some of the rice on each serving plate and transfer the beef and scallops from the skewers onto the plates next to the rice. Add 3 lobster slices to each plate and serve some of the sauce next to the meat, seafood, and rice. Garnish with the lemon slices and dill.

WINE SUGGESTION: *Red or white wine can be served with this dish; for example, a West Coast Pinot Noir or French Burgundy, or a California Sauvignon Blanc or Champagne.*

If you prefer, use linguine or another pasta of your choice instead of the rice. You can mix and match the "surf" part of this recipe as you wish: For example, you can use jumbo shrimp or shucked oysters instead of the lobster tails or scallops. Serve the beef and scallops on the skewers if you wish.

MERLE'S BARBECUED BEEF BRISKET WITH ALL THE FIXIN'S

Serves 6 to 8

Merle Ellis, known through his syndicated newspaper columns and by television fans as "The Butcher," is an old friend of ours, and this is a simple, finger-lickin' recipe for barbecued brisket. Merle is certainly well qualified on this subject; he has been awarded a Ph.B. (doctorate in barbecue) from the Kansas City Barbecue Society! His bestselling book, *Cutting Up in the Kitchen*, has sold almost 1 million copies, and this recipe is taken from his most recent opus, *The Great American Meat Book* (New York: Knopf, 1996). As Merle describes this brisket, "it's good, and it's hot!" Feel free to mix and match the "fixin's," adding or substituting your own favorites as you wish.

. . . .

To prepare the brisket, place the Worcestershire sauce, Tabasco sauce, butter, black pepper, red pepper, salt, and vinegar in a saucepan and bring to a boil. Turn down the heat and simmer for 10 minutes, stirring occasionally. Line a large roasting pan with foil and place the meat in it. Pour the sauce over the meat and fold the foil over to cover. Marinate in the refrigerator for 4 hours; remove from the refrigerator and bring to room temperature.

To prepare the salsa, place the bacon in a mixing bowl. Put the corn in a large sauté pan, add about ⅓ cup of water, and cook for 3 minutes over medium-high heat until the corn is tender and the liquid has evaporated. Transfer the corn to the bowl with the bacon. Add the

FOR THE BRISKET:

1 (10-ounce) bottle
  Worcestershire sauce
¼ cup Tabasco sauce
½ cup butter
1 tablespoon freshly
  ground black pepper
2 teaspoons dried red
  pepper flakes
1 tablespoon salt
2 cups cider vinegar
5 pounds beef brisket,
  choice grade

10 strips bacon, cooked
and diced

3 cups fresh corn kernels
(from 4 ears corn)

About ⅓ cup water

2 tablespoons cider
vinegar

1 red jalapeño chile,
thinly sliced, with
seeds

2 tablespoons olive oil

¼ teaspoon salt

½ teaspoon freshly
ground black pepper

1 recipe Drunken Beans
(page 10), or 1 recipe
Jalapeño Beans (page
67)

1 recipe Cheddar-
Poblano Corn Bread
(page 62) (optional)

vinegar, jalapeño, olive oil, salt, and pepper, and mix well. Keep refrigerated.

Preheat the oven to 325 degrees. Transfer the roasting pan to the oven and bake for 4 or 5 hours, or until very tender. For the last hour of cooking, fold the foil down to allow the meat to brown and soak up as much of the sauce as possible. Serve with the extra sauce on the side. (See page 211 for information on carving brisket.)

To prepare the rice, melt butter in a sauté pan and add the onion. Sauté over medium heat for 5 minutes. Add the cactus, and sauté for 5 minutes longer. Add the rice, pimentos, raisins, cinnamon, pineapple juice, and water, and bring to a boil. Continue to boil until the water has evaporated to the level of the rice; then reduce the heat to a simmer, cover the pan, and cook for about 15 minutes, stirring occasionally so that the rice does not stick to the bottom of the pan. When the water has evaporated but the rice is still moist, turn off the heat. Let the rice stand for 5 minutes and then fluff with a fork.

Serve the carved brisket family-style, with the beans, salsa, and rice in bowls and the corn bread stacked on a plate or in a basket.

WINE SUGGESTION:: *West Coast Pinot Noir works well with the barbecue flavors, as does a Cabernet Sauvignon from California.*

The colorful rice is given a sweetness by the cinnamon and fruit juice but contains no sugar. The raisins and cactus provide an interesting texture. Sliced cactus is often available in produce sections of supermarkets, especially in Latin neighborhoods, and whole cactus pads are usually sold in Latin markets. If using the latter, peel the cactus using thick leather gloves to make sure the spines don't get you! If you can't find cactus, or if you prefer, substitute 2 diced carrots and 1 diced stick of celery, add with the onion, and cook together for 10 minutes.

FOR THE CINNAMON-CACTUS RICE:

1 tablespoon butter

½ onion, finely diced

3 ounces nopales (cactus pads), diced (about ⅔ cup) (optional; see sidebar)

1 cup long-grain white rice, rinsed and drained

¼ cup bottled diced pimentos, drained

¼ cup seedless raisins

½ tablespoon ground cinnamon

1 cup pineapple juice

2 cups water

RED CHILE BEEF JERKY

Makes about 2 pounds

2 pounds beef top
   round, select grade or
   better
1 cup red chile powder
¼ cup kosher salt
¼ cup freshly ground
   black pepper

The technique of slowly drying meat in the sun or over open fires dates back centuries, when the Plains Indians made buffalo jerky and Native Americans of the Pacific Northwest preserved salmon. Of course, the technique was born of the necessity of keeping meat without the benefits of refrigeration, and many other cultures around the world developed similar methods. Following the advent of refrigeration, preserved meats were still used by hunters, hikers, and adventurers traveling for long periods. Today, we prepare jerky not out of necessity but because we enjoy the distinct flavor and texture that the curing and drying process brings. Flank steak also works well for this recipe.

Preheat the oven to 150 degrees or to its lowest setting.

To prepare the jerky, cut the beef with a knife or meat slicer with the grain into slices ¹⁄₁₆ to ⅛ inch thick. Combine the chile powder, salt, and pepper on a large platter and dredge the meat in the mixture until well covered. Place on racks set over 2 baking sheets and place in the oven overnight, or for 10 to 12 hours, until dry and chewy.

WINE SUGGESTION: *A dark beer goes well with jerky; as does a robust Pinot Noir from the West Coast.*

Making your own beef jerky is enjoyable and rewarding. Even when the meat has been purchased at your grocery store and baked in a slow oven rather than outdoors, there is still something profound about making jerky—perhaps the feeling of bringing us "back to the earth." It is an easy thing to make with older children (wear plastic gloves!) and it provides an excellent opportunity to teach them the history of preserving meat for survival. If thoroughly dried in the oven, jerky can be held indefinitely in a cool dry space. It can be eaten out of hand or chopped and added to salads, soups, and stews.

"RANCHERO" BEEF SALAD WITH LIME-CHIPOTLE DRESSING

Serves 4

This wonderful recipe is one of many in this book developed by Terry Finlayson, a talented food writer who attended Peter Kump's New York Cooking School before working in restaurants in New York and Puerto Rico. A former associate cookbook editor at the Culinary Institute of America, Terry writes on a freelance basis with the taste-testing assistance of her two children, Gabriel and Alanna. Terry's recipe assumes your picnic is taking place within reach of your kitchen (and of course, it's not meant just for picnics), but if you plan on taking this any distance, cook the beef and make the dressing ahead and keep them in separate containers. You will also want to roast the poblanos on the grill in advance, but the other ingredients can be taken whole and cut or sliced at the last minute.

....

To prepare the dressing, mix the chipotle, garlic, adobo sauce, lime juice, and vinegar in a bowl and mash to combine. Slowly whisk in the oils to incorporate. Season with salt and pepper and taste the dressing; add more minced chipotle if you prefer it hotter.

To prepare the dry rub, mix the chile powder, cumin, oregano, salt, and pepper in a small bowl. Lightly rub the mixture into the beef and let it sit in the refrigerator for about 1 hour. Meanwhile, prepare the grill.

Grill the steaks over medium-high heat for 3 to 4 minutes on each side for medium-rare, 4 to 5 minutes for medium, or to desired doneness. Remove the meat, let it

FOR THE LIME-CHIPOTLE DRESSING:

1 canned chipotle chile, minced

2 garlic cloves, minced

1 tablespoon adobo sauce (from canned chipotles)

3 tablespoons freshly squeezed lime juice

2 tablespoons white wine vinegar

¼ cup extra-virgin olive oil

¼ cup vegetable oil

Salt and freshly ground black pepper to taste

For the Dry Rub and Beef:

2 tablespoons pure red
 chile powder
2 teaspoons ground
 cumin
2 teaspoons dried
 oregano
½ teaspoon salt
¼ teaspoon freshly
 ground black pepper
3 strip sirloin steaks,
 prime or choice grade,
 about 10 ounces each
 and 1 inch thick

For the Salad:

1 head Romaine lettuce,
 torn into pieces
Lime-Chipotle Dressing
 (see previous page)
1 poblano chile, roasted,
 peeled, seeded, and
 sliced (page 208)
½ red onion, sliced
2 tomatoes, cut into
 wedges
12 yellow teardrop, pear,
 or cherry tomatoes
1 ripe avocado, peeled,
 pitted, and cut into
 large cubes
2 radishes, sliced
4 ounces blue cheese,
 crumbled
¼ cup pitted black olives,
 sliced
1 cup sour cream

rest for 5 minutes, and slice across the grain into ¼-inch-thick slices (the beef can also be served at room temperature).

To prepare the salad, place the lettuce in a mixing bowl and toss with about one quarter of the dressing, or enough to lightly coat the leaves. Spread the greens on a large serving platter. Arrange the sliced steak over the center of the lettuce. Arrange the poblano, onion, red and yellow tomatoes, and avocado around the steak. Sprinkle the radishes, cheese, and olives over the whole salad. Drizzle some of the dressing over the entire salad and serve any remaining dressing on the side, along with the sour cream. Serve your guests, or have them help themselves from the platter.

WINE SUGGESTION: *A French Burgundy from the northern region or a fine Pinot Noir from the West Coast will bring out the full character of this zesty dish.*

You may sauté the steak for about the same time described for grilling; we found that more of the rub flavor remained after cooking, although the smoky flavor from the grill was missing. Serve with a good, crusty French bread.

BEEF KEBABS WITH COUSCOUS SALAD

Serves 4

FOR THE MARINADE:

¼ cup red wine

¼ cup balsamic vinegar

¼ cup extra-virgin olive oil

1 tablespoon freshly squeezed lemon juice

1 tablespoon grated lemon zest

2 tablespoons freshly squeezed orange juice

1 tablespoon grated orange zest

3 garlic cloves, minced

1 teaspoon ground cumin

1 teaspoon salt

1 teaspoon freshly ground black pepper

Here's a recipe with a North African feel; you can almost sense the exotic sights and aromas of the Casbah as you prepare it. Couscous is made from semolina, and the packaged variety that is commonly available is precooked, making it quick and easy to prepare. While this dish may not be traditional fare for Labor Day, it's certainly ideal for a relaxed cookout. Strip steak gives a nice tender kebab, but any tender cut of beef, such as tenderloin tips or top sirloin, may be used.

Combine all the marinade ingredients in a large mixing bowl. Add the steak and marinate for at least 4 hours or overnight in the refrigerator. Drain the meat, reserving the marinade. Thread the beef, onions, mushrooms, tomatoes, sliced zucchini, and red bell pepper onto the skewers and lay them in a roasting pan. Pour the marinade over the kebabs and marinate for 1 hour longer.

Meanwhile, whisk together all the ingredients for the dressing in a small bowl and set aside. Place the couscous in a large mixing bowl; add the boiling water, cover, and let sit for 10 minutes. Fluff the couscous with a fork and let it cool slightly (about 5 minutes). Mix in the onion, scallion, currants, pumpkin seeds, apricots, and parsley. Stir in enough dressing to moisten the salad without making it soggy and let it sit for about 1 hour before serving. To serve, fluff again, and season with additional salt and lemon juice to taste.

Prepare the grill. About 15 minutes before serving, grill the kebabs for about 4 minutes on each side, or to the desired doneness. Serve with the couscous salad.

WINE SUGGESTION: *A West Coast Pinot Noir is our choice here, or a northern French Burgundy.*

FOR THE BEEF KEBABS:

1 ½ pounds boneless strip steaks, cut into 1½-inch cubes
2 sweet onions, quartered, then halved crosswise
8 mushrooms
8 cherry tomatoes
1 zucchini, cut in ¾-inch slices
1 red bell pepper, seeded and cut into 8 pieces
8 bamboo skewers, soaked in water for at least 30 minutes and drained

FOR THE COUSCOUS SALAD:

1¼ cups whole-wheat couscous
1 cup boiling water
¼ red onion, diced
1 scallion, sliced
¼ cup currants
¼ cup pumpkin seeds, toasted (page 210)
5 dried apricots, diced
2 to 3 teaspoons minced parsley (optional)
Lemon juice to taste

FOR THE COUSCOUS DRESSING:

3 tablespoons white wine vinegar
3 tablespoons extra-virgin olive oil
3 tablespoons freshly squeezed lemon juice
½ teaspoon cumin seeds, toasted and ground (page 209)
½ teaspoon coriander seeds, toasted and crushed (page 209)
¼ teaspoon ground cardamom
¼ teaspoon ground turmeric
⅛ teaspoon ground cinnamon
1 teaspoon salt

Whole-wheat couscous is available in many health food stores and gourmet markets. It has even more flavor and texture than regular couscous, but if it is not available, regular couscous may be substituted. The dressing can be made a day ahead and combined with the couscous just before serving.

GRILLED BLUE CHEESE AND MUSHROOM BURGERS WITH KATHY'S POTATO SALAD

Serves 4

FOR THE POTATO SALAD:

2 pounds Yukon Gold or
   Red Bliss potatoes,
   unpeeled and
   scrubbed
¼ cup cider vinegar
¼ cup chopped onion
1 garlic clove
½ cup olive oil
1 teaspoon sugar, or to
   taste
1 teaspoon Dijon
   mustard, or to taste
Salt and freshly ground
   pepper to taste
½ cup diced celery
1 bunch scallions,
   trimmed and sliced
2 tablespoons chopped
   Italian flat-leaf parsley

These burgers are not only delicious but also offer a fun surprise because the blue cheese is hidden inside the beef patties. The flavors of the blue cheese, beef, and mushrooms are a natural match. Our friend Kathy Long provided the potato salad recipe; Kathy, who used to work at the acclaimed Southwest restaurant Arizona 206 in New York City, is a private chef and an instructor at the Santa Fe School of Cooking.

Place the potatoes in a saucepan of salted water to cover and bring to a boil. Boil for 20 to 25 minutes or until just cooked through. Drain and with a very sharp knife cut into ¼-inch slices. Transfer to a mixing bowl. While the potatoes are cooking, place the vinegar, onion, garlic, and oil in a blender and puree. Season with the sugar, mustard, salt, and pepper. Pour the dressing over the warm potatoes in the mixing bowl and stir carefully to coat the slices without breaking them too much. Add the celery, scallions, and parsley, and stir to combine. Let the salad rest for 15 minutes, adjust the seasonings if necessary, and let cool to room temperature.

To prepare the mushrooms, heat the olive oil in a sauté pan and add the sliced mushrooms. Sauté over medium-high heat for 4 or 5 minutes, until golden brown. Keep warm.

To prepare the burgers, mix together the beef, salt, pepper, Worcestershire, Tabasco, onion, and parsley in a mixing bowl. Divide into 4 equal pieces and form with your hands into balls. Cut the cheese into 4 even squares or cubes, poke a hole into the center of each ball and insert the cheese. Re-form the balls and flatten to make patties. Heat the vegetable oil in a large nonstick sauté pan. Sear the burgers over medium-high heat for 1 minute on each side. Turn down the heat to medium and continue to cook for about 3 minutes per side, or until the internal temperature reaches 160 degrees (or medium).

Meanwhile, preheat the broiler. Split the hamburger buns and brush with the melted butter. Place under the broiler and toast briefly until golden brown. Place the beef patties on the bottom half of each bun on serving plates. Top the burgers with the mushrooms and serve open-faced with the potato salad on the side.

WINE SUGGESTION: *This zesty recipe deserves a hearty and robust Pinot Noir from the West Coast or a French Côtes-du-Rhône.*

If you prefer, serve the burgers with Shoestring Potatoes (page 17) instead of the potato salad. You may also serve with Drunken Beans (page 10) or Jalapeño Beans (page 67) if you like.

FOR THE MUSHROOMS:

2 tablespoons olive oil
6 ounces sliced mushrooms (about 2 cups)

FOR THE BURGERS:

1¼ pounds lean high-quality ground beef
Salt and freshly ground black pepper to taste
Dash of Worcestershire sauce
Dash of Tabasco sauce
½ cup minced onion
1 tablespoon minced parsley
2 ounces blue cheese
1 tablespoon vegetable oil
4 hamburger buns
2 tablespoons melted butter

3. RECIPES FOR FALL

RECIPES FOR SPECIAL OCCASIONS

**Russian Steppe Beef Borscht
with Meatballs, page 104**

PROVENÇALE TOP SIRLOIN STEAKS WITH TOMATOES AND OLIVES

Serves 4

For the Rosemary
Roasted Potatoes:

1½ pounds small Yukon
    Gold or red potatoes,
    unpeeled and
    scrubbed

5 garlic cloves, minced

3 tablespoons olive oil

1 teaspoon rosemary
    leaves

Salt and freshly ground
    black pepper to taste

This is a wonderfully flavorful and simple way of enjoying beef with early fall vegetables and a taste of the Mediterranean. You can cook this recipe with filet mignon if you prefer the richer flavor and silky texture; add a little extra cooking time to allow for the thicker steaks. This recipe is almost worth making just for the aroma of the roasting rosemary potatoes!

• •

Preheat the oven to 350 degrees.

Cut the potatoes into chunks and place in a baking dish or roasting pan with a 1-inch rim. Toss with the garlic, olive oil, and rosemary, and season with salt and pepper. Roast in the oven for about 1 hour, tossing occasionally, or until the potatoes are golden and crisp.

Meanwhile, prepare the steaks and vegetables. Heat 1 tablespoon of the oil in a large heavy skillet or sauté pan. Add the onion and garlic, and sauté over medium-high heat for 3 to 4 minutes, until softened. Remove from the pan and set aside. Heat another 1 tablespoon of the oil in the skillet, and add the remaining tablespoon of oil to a second skillet. Season the steaks with salt and pepper and add 2 to each skillet. Cook over high heat for 1½ minutes on each side, until browned. Push the steaks to one side of each skillet and divide the olives, celery, and zucchini between the 2 skillets. Cook for 2 minutes longer. Turn the steaks over and divide the tomatoes, sun-dried tomatoes, bell peppers, oregano, and vinegar between the 2 skillets. Add the reserved onion and garlic and cook for 2 minutes more for medium-rare (3 minutes for medium), stirring often. Transfer the steaks and vegetables to warm serving plates and serve with the roasted potatoes.

WINE SUGGESTION: *Côtes-du-Rhône or Beaujolais Villages from France, or a Pinot Noir from the West Coast, have just the right fruit and acidity to match this dish.*

FOR THE STEAKS AND VEGETABLES:

3 tablespoons olive oil

1 cup diced onion

3 garlic cloves, minced

4 top-sirloin steaks, prime or choice grade, about 7 ounces each and 1 inch thick

Salt and freshly ground black pepper to taste

½ cup (about 3 ounces) pitted Niçoise or other black olives

1 stalk celery, julienned

1 zucchini, julienned

3 Roma tomatoes, blanched, peeled, seeded, and julienned (page 207)

1 tablespoon minced sun-dried tomatoes (packed in oil)

2 red bell peppers, roasted, peeled, seeded, and julienned

1 tablespoon minced fresh oregano, or 1 teaspoon dried

2 tablespoons white wine vinegar

To save the effort of roasting the bell peppers, you can use bottled whole roasted peppers available at gourmet stores and in Greek and Middle Eastern stores.

NEW MEXICO BEEF STEW WITH GREEN CHILES AND POSOLE

Serves 4 to 6

This classic Southwestern dish is traditional fare during the fall, especially for family gatherings and holiday season celebrations. The long green chiles grown in the Rio Grande Valley in the southern part of New Mexico, especially around Hatch, are among the most flavorful in the world, and with a medium heat, they are popular in many regional recipes. Posole is the Spanish name for field corn that has been treated with slaked lime to remove the tough outer layer of the kernels, similar to hominy. Posole is also the name given to a stew made with pork and posole corn, but beef, lamb, and goat work equally well. Serve this stew with warm flour tortillas, fresh crusty bread, or corn bread (page 62).

....

Heat 2 tablespoons of the olive oil in a large saucepan or stockpot. Place the flour in a shallow bowl or on a large plate and season with salt and pepper. Dredge the beef in the flour, add half to the saucepan, and sear over medium-high heat for about 5 minutes, or until browned on all sides. Remove the beef from the pan with a slotted spoon. Heat the remaining 1 tablespoon of olive oil and repeat for the remaining beef. Add the first batch back to the pan when the second batch has cooked. Add the beef stock, water, and wine, and bring to a boil. Add the posole, onion, garlic, and green chiles, and return to a boil. Reduce the heat to a simmer and add the cumin, oregano, salt, and pepper. Cook, partially covered, for 1½ hours, stirring occasionally.

Add the potatoes and carrots, and continue to cook for 1 hour or until the potatoes and posole are tender and the kernels have opened up. Add a little more water if necessary to keep the consistency soupy, and adjust the seasonings as necessary.

WINE SUGGESTION: *This stew demands a wine of strong character as well. The Rhône Valley of France provides just such wines: Châteauneuf-du-Pape, Gigondas, St. Joseph, and Hermitage are all good choices.*

You can use dried posole in this recipe, but the stew will take up to 5 hours to cook. If using dried posole, add the potatoes 1 hour before the stew finishes cooking. If posole is unavailable, use canned (precooked) hominy. Rinse it well and add 15 minutes from the end of the cooking process.

3 tablespoons olive oil

1 cup all-purpose flour

Salt and freshly ground black pepper to taste

1 pound top-sirloin or chuck steak, choice grade, cut into ½-inch dice

3 cups Beef Stock (page 200)

2 cups water

1 cup red wine

1 pound fresh posole, rinsed

1 onion, diced

5 garlic cloves, minced

5 New Mexico green chiles, or green Anaheim chiles, roasted, peeled, seeded, and diced (page 208)

1 teaspoon ground cumin

1 tablespoon dried oregano

¾ teaspoon salt, or to taste

1 teaspoon freshly ground black pepper

2 russet potatoes, about 8 ounces each, chopped

2 carrots, sliced

RUSSIAN STEPPE BEEF BORSCHT WITH MEATBALLS

Serves 8

FOR THE MEATBALLS:

1 tablespoon butter

½ onion, minced

1 garlic clove, minced

½ teaspoon chopped thyme

12 ounces lean high-quality ground beef

¼ cup fresh bread crumbs

1 egg, beaten

Salt and freshly ground black pepper to taste

4 cups Beef Stock (page 200)

Borscht is a beet soup originating in Eastern Europe. Although it always contains beets, the meat, stock, and vegetables vary from region to region. This version, with meatballs rather than diced meat, is a favorite in the Russian Steppe region, the vast treeless grassland prairie. Borscht may be served hot (as it is here) or chilled, and is traditionally garnished with a dollop of sour cream. If serving this recipe chilled, you can puree it, but since the meatballs go best with warm borscht, you might want to omit them from the chilled version. Serve with a good crusty bread.

· ·

To prepare the meatballs, melt the butter in a stockpot or large saucepan, add the onion, and sauté over medium heat for about 5 minutes, or until softened. Add the garlic and thyme and sauté for 2 minutes longer; transfer to a large mixing bowl and let cool. Add the beef, bread crumbs, and egg to the bowl and gently mix to combine. Season with salt and pepper. Form into 16 meatballs and refrigerate for about 30 minutes. In a saucepan, bring the stock to a boil, turn down the heat to a simmer, and add the meatballs (in batches, if necessary) and cook for about 15 minutes, or until no longer pink, occasionally skimming the surface of the stock to remove any impurities. Remove the meatballs from the broth with a slotted spoon and keep warm, or refrigerate until ready to serve. Discard the broth. If refrigerating, reheat the meatballs in a low oven or in 1 cup of fresh broth.

For the Borscht:

6 beets, well scrubbed

3 tablespoons butter

1 onion, diced

2 carrots, diced

1 leek, diced

1 garlic clove, minced

2 tablespoons red wine vinegar

6 cups Beef Stock (page 200)

1 Idaho potato (about 8 ounces), peeled and diced

½ head small cabbage (about 1 pound), diced

2 bay leaves

Salt and freshly ground black pepper to taste

½ teaspoon chopped thyme

½ cup sour cream, for garnish

1 teaspoon minced parsley, for garnish

To prepare the borscht, cut the greens off the beets, leaving about 1 inch of stem. Place the beets in a saucepan with just enough cold water to cover, and bring to a boil. Turn down the heat and simmer, partially covered, for 30 to 40 minutes, or until tender. Remove the beets, and reserve 1 of them. Peel and dice the remaining 5 beets; there should be about 4 cups. Reserve the cooking liquid.

Heat the butter in a stockpot or large saucepan, add the onion, and sauté over medium heat 5 to 7 minutes, or until softened. Add the carrots, leek, garlic, and diced beets and sauté for 2 to 3 minutes longer. Stir in the vinegar and cook for 1 minute, while stirring the bottom of the pan. Pour in 6 cups of the beef stock and the cooking liquid from the beets, and add the potato, cabbage, and bay leaves. Season with salt and pepper. Bring to a boil, skim the surface to remove any impurities, and turn the heat down to medium-low. Simmer for about 45 minutes, skimming the surface occasionally.

Remove the bay leaves and transfer 1 cup of the soup and vegetables to a blender. Dice the reserved beet and add to the blender. Puree and add the mixture back to the soup. Add up to 2 cups more stock or water if the soup gets too thick. Add the thyme a few minutes before you are ready to serve. Season with additional salt, pepper, and red wine vinegar as necessary.

Ladle the warm soup into serving bowls and add 2 meatballs to each serving. Garnish with a dollop of sour cream and the parsley.

WINE SUGGESTION: *Merlot is the choice here as a tasty complement to the flavorful mixture of ingredients. St. Émilion, from Bordeaux (the original progenitor of Californian Merlots), would be equally appropriate.*

We used the paysanne cut for the beets, carrots, and potatoes; this is a ½-inch square about ¼ inch thick. This takes a bit more time, but gives an attractive appearance to the soup. Whether you dice the vegetables, or cut them in paysanne, try to keep them a uniform size.

Although this recipe calls for 6 beets, the amount of beets you need will vary depending on size. You may need as few as 4 large or as many as 8 small. Don't be dismayed if you don't have exactly 4 cups of diced beets. A little more or less won't affect the flavor of the soup, and by adding the cooking broth to the soup, you will achieve the intense purple color of borscht.

SANTA FE-STYLE COTTAGE PIE WITH RED CHILE–MASHED POTATO TOPPING

Serves 4 to 6

In this recipe, the classic English cottage pie is enlivened by a zingy (rather than plain) red chile topping. Don't be put off by this description of cottage pie's near kin, shepherd's pie (made with lamb) given in *Great British Cooking* (subtitle: *A Well-Kept Secret*), by Jane Garmey (HarperCollins, 1992): "Shepherd's Pie has always been a favorite standby for institutional cooks and has been forced unwillingly on successive generations of schoolchildren, prison inmates, and paying guests in seaside establishments of dubious quality." We promise, this recipe won't remind you of that description. In fact, it's downright delicious and a quick and easy way to feed hungry guests or family.

....

Heat the olive oil in a saucepan and sauté the garlic, onion, leeks, and carrots over medium-high heat for 5 minutes. Add the beef and sauté for 7 or 8 minutes longer, while stirring frequently, or until the beef is well browned on all sides. Season with salt and pepper. Add the flour and cook for 1 minute longer. Add the stock, wine, tomato paste, Worcestershire sauce, and dried herbs. Reduce the heat to medium and cook, uncovered, for 30 minutes, stirring occasionally. Stir in the peas and remove from the heat.

Transfer the mixture to a large ovenproof glass baking dish, preferably 9 or 10 inches square, and let cool while preparing the mashed potatoes. Meanwhile, preheat the oven to 350 degrees.

FOR THE PIE:

2 tablespoons olive oil

2 garlic cloves, minced

1 large onion, sliced

2 leeks (green and white parts), sliced and chopped (about 2 cups)

2 carrots, sliced

1 ½ pounds lean high-quality ground beef

Salt and freshly ground black pepper

1 tablespoon flour

1 cup Beef Stock (page 200)

½ cup white wine

3 tablespoons tomato paste

2 teaspoons Worcestershire sauce

1 teaspoon mixed dried herbs, such as Herbes de Provence

1 cup frozen peas

For the Topping:
1 recipe Red Chile
Mashed Potatoes (page
57)

With a fork, spread the mashed potatoes evenly over the beef mixture, making a ridged pattern on the top of the potatoes with the fork. Bake in the oven for 25 minutes. Place under the preheated broiler and broil the top of the potatoes until golden brown, about 2 to 3 minutes. Let cool slightly before serving.

Wine Suggestion: *The zing of this recipe suggests a Spanish red, preferably from the Rioja or Penedès regions. Alternatively, try a Beaujolais from France.*

Traditionally, cottage pie and shepherd's pie are ideal recipes for using up leftover beef or lamb that is then minced, but you won't need an excuse like leftovers to make this dish with store-bought freshly ground beef. If you prefer, for a plainer topping, mash boiled potatoes with butter and milk and sprinkle in ½ cup of grated Cheddar cheese. Spread the potatoes over the beef and bake in the oven for 30 minutes.

JAMES BEARD'S MARINATED ENTRECÔTE GAUCHO STEAKS WITH WHEAT PILAF

Serves 4

Here is another recipe that we have adapted from a combination suggested by the late James Beard. *Entrecôte* is a French term that refers to a specific cut of tender steak between the ribs, which is essentially the same as the boneless strip steaks we use in this recipe. Jim probably named these steaks "gaucho" to evoke the spirit of the pampas-riding South American cowboys who undoubtedly grilled their steak over open fires.

....

To prepare the marinade, combine the scallions, wine, vinegar, salt, and pepper in a mixing bowl. Place the steaks in a dish or bowl and pour the marinade over. Let the steaks marinate overnight, or for at least 4 hours.

Prepare the grill (alternatively, the steaks may be broiled).

To prepare the pilaf, place the bulghur in a fine-mesh sieve, rinse under cold running water, and drain. Heat the butter over medium-high heat in a saucepan and add the garlic, onion, and celery. Sauté for 2 minutes and then add the mushrooms. Sauté for 2 minutes longer, stirring well. Add the oregano and bulghur, continuing to stir well. Add the stock, salt, and pepper. Cover the pan and simmer for about 25 minutes or until the bulghur has absorbed the liquid, stirring occasionally.

While the pilaf is cooking, remove the steaks from the marinade, reserving the marinade. Grill the steaks over medium-high heat for about 3 minutes on each side for

For the Marinade and Steaks:

2 cups sliced scallions
1 cup white wine
⅓ cup champagne vinegar
1 teaspoon salt
1 tablespoon freshly ground black pepper
4 boneless strip-sirloin steaks, prime or choice grade, about 9 ounces each and 1 inch thick

For the Wheat Pilaf:

1 cup bulghur

3 tablespoons butter

1 tablespoon minced
garlic

½ cup diced onion

½ cup diced celery

1 cup sliced mushrooms,
about 3 ounces

½ teaspoon minced
oregano or marjoram

2 cups chicken stock

Salt and freshly ground
black pepper to taste

For the Tarragon Butter Sauce (optional):

Reserved marinade (see
previous page)

¼ cup butter

2 teaspoons minced
tarragon

1 avocado, peeled, pitted,
and thinly sliced, for
garnish

medium-rare, about 4 minutes on each side for medium, or to desired doneness.

To prepare the sauce, bring the marinade to a boil in a saucepan. Turn down the heat to a simmer and cook for 7 or 8 minutes. Stir in the butter and tarragon.

Serve the steaks with the pilaf and pour the sauce over the steaks. Garnish with the sliced avocado.

Wine Suggestion: *California Cabernet Sauvignon or a French Bordeaux.*

Bulghur wheat, popular in Middle Eastern cuisine, is steamed, dried, and crushed wheat. It makes a tender and delicious pilaf. If broiling the steaks, we recommend searing them in a hot skillet first, about 1 minute on each side, and then broiling for about the same time as called for in this recipe.

CUBAN ROPA VIEJA WITH FRIED PLANTAINS AND RICE

Serves 4

This Latin recipe, brought to the New World from Spain centuries ago, is like a beef hash with a lot of soul. It is a dish that is common in Central and South America and the Caribbean, and there are many versions; this one is Cuban. There are many theories as to the origin of the name "Ropa Vieja," literally "old clothes." One suggests that the shredded beef resembles rags; another, that leftover beef can be used—a hand-me-down recipe turning old clothes (or beef) into new.

....

To prepare the Ropa Vieja, place the water, garlic, onions, carrots, celery, jalapeños, peppercorns, juniper berries, thyme, bay leaves, and salt in a large saucepan and bring to a boil. Reduce the heat and simmer for 10 minutes. Add the steak, cover the pan, and cook over low heat for 2 hours or until the beef is tender. Remove the meat and set aside. Let the broth cool. When the beef is cool enough, using your fingers, shred with the grain into 3- or 4-inch lengths and set aside.

To prepare the sauce, heat the oil in a saucepan, add the garlic and onion, and sauté over medium heat for 2 minutes. Add the oregano, bay leaves, tomato paste, wine, vinegar, 1 cup of the cooled beef broth, and season with salt and pepper. Cook for 10 minutes and then add the bell peppers and shredded beef. Turn down the heat to low and simmer for 15 minutes longer. Remove the bay leaves.

To prepare the plantains, mix together the pepper,

For the Ropa Vieja:

3 quarts water
6 garlic cloves
2 onions, cut into quarters
2 carrots, sliced
3 stalks celery, chopped
2 jalapeño chiles, chopped
1 teaspoon black peppercorns
1 teaspoon juniper berries
4 sprigs thyme
2 bay leaves
1 teaspoon salt
1½ pounds skirt steak or flank steak, select grade or better, cut into 2 or 3 strips

For the Sauce:

2 tablespoons olive oil

2 garlic cloves, minced

1 onion, diced

½ teaspoon dried oregano

1 bay leaf

¼ cup tomato paste

½ cup white wine

2 tablespoons
    champagne vinegar

1 cup cooled beef broth
    (see previous page)

Salt and freshly ground
    black pepper to taste

1 green bell pepper,
    roasted, peeled,
    seeded, and diced
    (page 208)

1 red bell pepper,
    roasted, peeled,
    seeded, and diced
    (page 208)

salt, cumin, and cinnamon in a bowl. Lay the plantain slices on a work surface and sprinkle on one side only with the spice mixture. Heat ⅛ inch of the vegetable oil in a sauté pan over medium-high heat and place the plantain slices, spice side down, in the hot oil. Cook for about 2 minutes per side or until golden brown or slightly black. Remove the slices and drain on paper towels. Keep warm.

Serve the ropa vieja and sauce with the rice and garnish with the fried plantains, spice side up.

Wine Suggestion: *Food with a Spanish or Latino soul requires the fitting complement—a Spanish Rioja. Italian Bardolino also works well here.*

The rest of the broth in which the beef cooked can be strained and used for stock or as a base for soup (just add fresh vegetables). The plantain recipe is from our good friend Norman Van Aken, owner of the wildly popular and acclaimed restaurant, Norman's, in Coral Gables, Florida. As an alternative to the plantains, serve cooked black beans or another bean recipe from this book.

FOR THE PLANTAINS:

1 teaspoon freshly
   ground black pepper

¼ teaspoon salt

½ teaspoon ground
   cumin

½ teaspoon ground
   cinnamon

2 ripe plantains, peeled
   and cut on a diagonal
   into ¼-inch slices

Vegetable oil, for frying

1 recipe Long-Grain
   White Rice (page 205)

DIJONNAISE BOEUF À LA BOURGIGNONNE WITH SOUR CREAM–GRATIN POTATOES

Serves 4 to 6

This classic beef stew from Burgundy is named for Dijon, the gateway to that famous French wine-growing region. Since medieval times, Dijon has perhaps been best known as the center of the mustard industry, and it is also a city renowned for its hearty food, such as this dish. For best results, don't stint on the wine; there really is a direct correlation between the quality of the wine and the flavors of the finished dish. Gratin potatoes are our favorite choice as an accompaniment, but alternatively, you can serve rice, or plenty of crusty French bread to mop up the deliciously rich sauce.

....

Preheat the oven to 325 degrees.

Heat 1 tablespoon of the olive oil in a heavy ovenproof casserole or large ovenproof saucepan and add the bacon. Sauté over medium-high heat for about 5 minutes or until golden brown. Remove with a slotted spoon and drain on paper towels. Add the onions and cook, while stirring frequently, for about 5 minutes longer, or until light golden brown. Remove and drain on paper towels. Heat the remaining tablespoon of olive oil and the butter in the casserole. Place the flour in a shallow bowl or on a large plate and season with salt and pepper. Dredge the beef in the flour and add to the casserole in 2 or 3 batches. Sear over medium-high heat for about 5 minutes, or until browned on all sides. Return all the meat to the casserole, add the sautéed bacon and onions, and add the garlic. Cook for 2 minutes, while stirring. Add the wine, stock, water, and tomato paste and scrape the bottom of the pan with a wooden spoon to incorporate any drippings.

Tie together the thyme, parsley, bay leaves, lemon zest, and celery (or place inside a piece of cheesecloth and tie to secure) and add to the casserole. Bring to a boil, stirring frequently, and season with salt and pepper. Cover the casserole and cook in the oven for 2 hours, or until the beef is tender. Add the mushrooms, stir well, and cook for 30 minutes longer. Remove the tied herbs and serve.

About 1 hour before you are ready to serve, prepare the potatoes. Serve with the beef.

WINE SUGGESTION: *Use the same wine that you added to the recipe: French Burgundy or a West Coast Pinot Noir.*

> Leave as much of the root end on the onions as possible as they will hold together better during the cooking process. If button mushrooms are unavailable, cut larger mushrooms in half or even into quarters.

2 tablespoons olive oil

6 ounces bacon slices, diced (about 1½ cups)

8 ounces pearl or boiling onions, trimmed

1 tablespoon butter

1 cup all-purpose flour

Salt and freshly ground black pepper to taste

1½ pounds top-round or chuck steak, choice grade, trimmed and cut into ¾-inch dice

3 garlic cloves, minced

2 cups Burgundy red wine, or Pinot Noir (see wine suggestion)

1 cup Beef Stock (page 200)

1 cup water

1½ tablespoons tomato paste

3 sprigs thyme

3 sprigs parsley or marjoram

2 bay leaves

1 strip lemon zest, 1 to 2 inches long

1 strip celery, 1 to 2 inches long

8 ounces button mushrooms, cleaned

Sour Cream–Gratin Potatoes (page 25)

CANTONESE BEEF IN OYSTER SAUCE WITH WOOD EAR MUSHROOM FRIED RICE

Serves 4

FOR THE BEEF AND MARINADE:

1 pound top-sirloin steak, prime or choice grade, cut into thin strips about 1 inch long and ⅛ inch thick

Freshly ground black pepper to taste

1 tablespoon light soy sauce

1 teaspoon sugar

2 tablespoons dry sherry

1 egg, beaten

2 teaspoons minced ginger

Canton is a province in southern China with a subtropical climate, and its diverse agriculture and extensive coastline have contributed to a long tradition of sophisticated flavors and technique. The Cantonese style of cooking is perhaps the best known of all the Chinese cuisines in the United States because most of the early immigrants came from that province. The rice dish is substantial enough to be a main course on its own if you double all the ingredients.

Season the beef with pepper, place in a mixing bowl, and add the soy sauce, sugar, sherry, egg, and ginger. Mix well and let marinate for 30 minutes.

To prepare the rice, soak the mushrooms in a bowl of warm water for 20 minutes. When rehydrated, cut off the stems and dice. Heat 2 tablespoons of the oil in a wok. Add the ginger and onion, and stir-fry over medium-high heat for 3 minutes. Add the mushroom stems and caps, and stir-fry for 2 minutes longer. Add the salt, sugar, and soy sauce, and stir-fry for 1 minute longer. Add the rice and stir-fry for 2 minutes or until warmed through. Heat the remaining tablespoon of oil in another wok or large sauté pan. Season the eggs with salt and pepper and gently stir-fry for about 1 to 2 minutes, or until just set. Add the peas and stir-fry for 1½ minutes longer. Add to the rice mixture and mix well. Transfer to a warm serving bowl and keep warm.

For the stir-fry, heat the oil in a clean wok until just

smoking. Mix 1 tablespoon of the cornstarch and flour in a small bowl. Remove the beef from the marinade and dredge in the cornstarch and flour mixture. Stir-fry in the oil over high heat for 2 minutes. Remove and drain on paper towels.

Pour off the remaining oil, leaving 2 tablespoons. Reheat the wok, add the snow peas, and stir-fry over medium-high heat for 1 ½ minutes. Remove with a slotted spoon and place on serving plates, forming a bed. In a small bowl, mix together the soy sauce, ketchup, Worcestershire sauce, oyster sauce, water, and sugar. Add to the pan, stir in the remaining ½ tablespoon of cornstarch and the ginger, and bring to a boil. Add the reserved beef and stir-fry for 1 minute, coating the beef with the sauce. Remove and arrange on top of the bed of snow peas. Garnish with the scallions and serve with the rice.

FOR THE RICE:

¼ cup dried wood ear (Chinese) mushrooms (about ½ ounce)

3 tablespoons vegetable oil

½ teaspoon minced ginger

1 large onion, finely sliced

Pinch of salt

1 teaspoon sugar

1 tablespoon light soy sauce

1 recipe Long-Grain White Rice (page 205; see sidebar, below)

2 eggs, lightly beaten

Salt and freshly ground black pepper to taste

¼ cup frozen peas

FOR THE STIR-FRY:

⅓ cup vegetable oil

1½ tablespoons cornstarch

1 tablespoon all-purpose flour

8 ounces snow peas, trimmed

1 tablespoon light soy sauce

1 tablespoon tomato ketchup

1 tablespoon Worcestershire sauce

2 tablespoons oyster sauce

1 tablespoon water

1 teaspoon sugar

1 teaspoon minced ginger

3 scallions, sliced (about ¼ cup), for garnish

WINE SUGGESTION: *The combination of soy sauce and ginger calls for a very sturdy wine such as a Cabernet Sauvignon, either from the Médoc area of Bordeaux or the Napa or Sonoma valleys of California.*

The trick with this recipe is to prepare the ingredients ahead of time—cut, dice, and measure out—or what in professional cooking is termed *mise-en-place*. For 2 cups of cooked white rice, begin with ¾ cup dry rice.

Oyster sauce is thick and dark brown, made with soy sauce and oysters. It is used most commonly in the cuisines of southern China.

Ideally, this recipe should be prepared in 2 woks. If you own only one, prepare the eggs and vegetables in a sauté pan.

BLACK PEPPER–CRUSTED ANGUS SIRLOIN STEAK WITH A SHIITAKE MUSHROOM SAUCE

Serves 4

FOR THE STEAKS:

½ cup olive oil

2 garlic cloves, mashed

12 basil leaves, minced

Salt to taste

2 tablespoons freshly
cracked black pepper

4 boneless Angus strip
steaks, prime or choice
grade, 10 ounces each
(or other high-quality
strip steaks)

This recipe is contributed by our friend Lionel Havé, executive chef at the Omaha Country Club. Lionel was born in France, where he served his culinary apprenticeship, before moving on to the Bahamas to open the King's Inn Hotel and later to Dallas, where he worked at the renowned Mansion on Turtle Creek. After working on restaurant projects in Cincinnati owned by Pete Rose and Boomer Esiason, Lionel took his current position in 1988. Black Angus cattle were introduced to the United States from their native Aberdeenshire in Scotland toward the end of the nineteenth century, and their numbers account for 20 percent of the beef breeds in the United States. Angus cattle have a reputation for yielding high-quality beef with very favorable marbling (and, therefore, flavor).

· ·

Pour the olive oil into a large glass dish or shallow bowl and combine with the garlic, basil, salt, and pepper. Rub this mixture into the steaks and marinate for 24 hours, turning occasionally.

Preheat the oven to 350 degrees. Bake the Idaho potatoes in the oven for about 1 hour, or until tender. Remove, split open lengthwise, scoop out the flesh, and reserve for another meal. Set the potato skins aside.

While the Idaho potatoes are baking, place the Red Bliss potatoes in a large saucepan of salted water and bring to a boil. Turn down the heat and simmer for about 20 minutes, or until tender. Drain the potatoes and return to the saucepan, stirring them over medium-high heat for 1 minute so they are dry. Add the milk, sour cream, butter, and cheese, and whisk or mash with a fork, leaving the potatoes a little chunky. Season with nutmeg, salt, and pepper and fill the potato skins with the mixture. Keep warm.

Prepare the grill.

While the potatoes are cooking, prepare the sauce. Melt the butter in a skillet over medium heat, add the mushrooms, and sauté for 3 minutes. Add the shallots and cook for 1 minute longer. Add the wine and bourbon, and reduce the liquid until it has evaporated. Add the cream and stock, and reduce until the consistency is syrupy, 10 to 15 minutes. Season with salt and pepper.

Remove the steaks from the marinade and grill over high heat for about 4 minutes on each side for medium-rare, about 5 minutes on each side for medium, or to the desired doneness. Transfer to warm serving plates and add a filled potato half to each plate. Spoon the sauce around each plate and garnish with the chives.

WINE SUGGESTION: *A northern Italian wine, such as Barolo, Barbaresco, or Gattinara, or a Petite Syrah from California.*

Use the flesh from the baking potatoes for another purpose. For example, add a little butter and milk, and mash them; keep refrigerated and use with another meal.

FOR THE POTATOES:

2 Idaho baking potatoes, 8 to 10 ounces each

1½ pounds Red Bliss potatoes, scrubbed and quartered

¼ cup warm milk

½ cup sour cream, at room temperature

¼ cup butter, at room temperature

6 tablespoons freshly grated Parmesan cheese

Nutmeg, to taste

Salt and pepper to taste

FOR THE SHIITAKE SAUCE:

¼ cup butter

8 large shiitake mushrooms, sliced

2 tablespoons finely minced shallots

1 cup white wine

¼ cup bourbon

1 cup heavy cream

½ cup Beef Stock (page 200)

Salt and freshly ground black pepper to taste

2 teaspoons sliced chives, for garnish

SCOTCH COLLOPS WITH HERBED BREAD DUMPLINGS

Serves 4

FOR THE COLLOPS:

12 ounces chuck steak, choice grade, or skirt steak, select grade or better

12 ounces lamb leg meat (or 12 additional ounces of chuck steak)

Salt and freshly ground black pepper to taste

1 tablespoon olive oil

1 tablespoon butter

1 onion, sliced

8 ounces button mushrooms, sliced

2 garlic cloves, minced

¼ cup sherry

2 cups Beef Stock (page 200)

1 cup heavy cream

Collops is the Scottish term (originally from Scandinavia) for what the French call escalope and the Italians commonly call scaloppine—thin, flattened slices of meat. Early recipes call for venison or other game, but today, the dish can range from minced meats to recipes such as this one, which uses sliced beef and lamb. The lamb in our recipe provides a hint of the game flavor; however, all beef may be used if you prefer. A crisp green salad goes very well with this dish.

• •

To prepare the collops, cut the meat into ¼-inch-thick slices about 2 inches by 5 inches. Pound the meat lightly for about 1 minute with a meat mallet or rolling pin and season with salt and pepper. Heat the oil in a large saucepan and sear the meat, in batches, over medium-high heat for about 1 minute on each side. Remove the collops as they are finished and arrange on the bottom of a baking pan or large casserole.

Reduce the heat to medium, add the butter to the pan, and sauté the onion for about 7 minutes, or until translucent. Add the mushrooms and sauté for about 3 minutes, or until they are softened but not cooked through. Add the garlic and cook for 2 minutes longer until softened. Raise the heat to medium-high, stir in the sherry, and reduce by half, about 3 to 4 minutes. Add the beef stock and reduce by half, about 10 to 15 minutes. Turn down the heat to medium, add the heavy cream, and simmer until the sauce is reduced to the consistency of heavy cream, about 5 to 6 minutes. Season with salt and pepper to taste. Pour the sauce over the meat and set aside.

Preheat the oven to 350 degrees.

To prepare the dumplings, place the bread and eggs in a bowl and toss gently to combine. Stir in the parsley, thyme, salt, and pepper. Let this mixture sit for 5 minutes. Stir the bread again and let it sit for 5 more minutes. Mix in the softened butter to incorporate; do not overmix or the butter will melt. Chill the mixture for at least 15 minutes. Shape the dough into balls. Heat the oil in a nonstick pan and sear the balls over medium-low heat for 6 or 7 minutes or until firm and golden brown all around (if they brown too quickly, reduce the heat, cover the pan, and continue cooking).

Place the bread dumplings on top of the sauce and collops and heat in the oven just until the dish is heated through, about 10 minutes. Remove from the oven and sprinkle freshly cracked black pepper over the top.

WINE SUGGESTION: *Gamay Beaujolais from California or one of the lighter Beaujolais Villages from France. Or, for a little adventure, try a Tavel Rosé from southern France.*

FOR THE DUMPLINGS:

8 slices "day old" white bread, crusts removed, diced (about 3 cups)
2 eggs, beaten
4 teaspoons chopped parsley
2 teaspoons chopped thyme
½ teaspoon salt
1 teaspoon freshly ground black pepper
¼ cup butter, slightly softened and diced
2 tablespoons vegetable oil

Use a tender cut of beef; chuck or skirt steak works best. Buy lamb slices cut from the leg, if available. Although traditionally, the dumplings are boiled, we have sautéed them here to give them a crisp texture, which contrasts well with the creamy sauce. You may substitute 2 ounces of minced suet for the butter in the bread dumplings.

BEEF SUKIYAKI
Serves 4

FOR THE SUKIYAKI:

2 ounces cellophane
    noodles

3 tablespoons suet or
    peanut oil

6 scallions, cut into 1-
    inch slices

10 shiitake mushrooms
    (about 8 ounces)

8 ounces Chinese
    cabbage, thinly sliced

4 ounces snow peas (or
    sliced bamboo shoots
    or bean sprouts)

2 tablespoons sugar

Sukiyaki is a Japanese stir-fry that is traditionally prepared at the table in a special pan. Guests use chopsticks to serve themselves out of the pan or to cook the meat in the simmering broth, as with fondue. This recipe has been adapted so that it can be prepared quickly in your kitchen. It uses trefoil, a member of the parsley family, which has a long thin stem with many 3-pointed leaves. It has a light flavor somewhat similar to sorrel or celery. Trefoil can be found in some Asian markets but if it is not available, use 3 ounces of sorrel or spinach.

· ·

Cook the noodles *al dente,* according to the package directions. Rinse under cold water and cut into 2-inch lengths.

Heat half of the suet in a large heavy sauté pan or wok over medium-high heat until it begins to melt. Cooking the ingredients in 2 batches, add half of the scallions, mushrooms, cabbage, and snow peas, and toss to coat with the hot fat. Stir in half of the sugar and caramelize the vegetables for about 2 minutes. Push the vegetables to the side and add some of the beef in 1 layer; sear until browned on all sides, about 1 to 2 minutes, and then push it aside as it cooks and add more of the beef until you have used half of it; do not overcook. Add $\frac{1}{4}$ cup each of sake and soy sauce, about 1 cup of the stock, and half of the tofu. Bring to a boil. Turn down the heat to medium-low, add half of the noodles and trefoil, and simmer briefly, until the vegetables are just cooked, about 2 to 3 minutes. Keep warm while you prepare the second batch, repeating the process. Serve in warm bowls with the rice on the side.

WINE SUGGESTION: *Serve a robust Pinot Noir from the West Coast, or Japanese plum wine for those with a sweet tooth.*

Cellophane noodles are called for in this recipe, but traditionally, shiratake—a thin starchy noodle made from a root vegetable—is used. Shiratake is hard to find unless you have a good Japanese market nearby. One option with this recipe is to double the amount of noodles and omit the rice.

Suet is a little-used ingredient these days, but it gives the dish a richness that the oil does not. Traditionally, raw egg is used with sukiyaki, as a dip; it cooks immediately on contact with the hot food. However, due to health concerns, the egg is often omitted and it is not recommended if you are preparing the dish in your kitchen to bring to the table. If you prefer to omit the tofu, add more beef or vegetables.

1½ pounds top sirloin, prime or choice grade, very thinly sliced

½ cup sake

½ cup soy sauce

2 cups Beef Stock (page 200), or more as necessary

8 ounces firm tofu

1 bunch trefoil (3 ounces of leaves)

Short-Grain Sticky Rice (page 204)

JAMES BEARD'S ROQUEFORT-BROILED STEAKS WITH WATERCRESS-MESCLUN SALAD

Serves 4

FOR THE SHERRY
VINAIGRETTE:
½ teaspoon Dijon
    mustard
½ teaspoon minced
    shallot
¼ cup sherry vinegar
¼ cup olive oil
2 tablespoons walnut oil
Salt and freshly ground
    black pepper to taste

The late, great James Beard recommended a 3-inch-thick sir-loin for this hearty recipe, but we prefer to use a 1½-inch-thick steak, which gives us more surface area on which to spread the Roquefort. Jim also recommended a baked potato and a "lusty red Burgundy" and we can't argue with that. The water-cress salad, which is our creation, pairs the Roquefort with pears and walnuts, two favorite accompaniments for blue cheese. The sharp watercress and tart but sweet vinaigrette complement the rich beef and Roquefort very well.

To prepare the vinaigrette, mix the mustard, shallot, and vinegar in a small bowl. Whisk in the olive oil and walnut oil, and season with salt and pepper. Set aside and whisk just before serving.

Cream the Roquefort, butter, Worcestershire sauce, and chives together in a mixing bowl. Season the steaks with pepper. Heat a nonstick pan over medium-high heat and sear the steaks for about 1 ½ minutes on the first side until they are nicely browned. Turn and sear on the other side for 1 ½ minutes. Turn down the heat to medium and continue to cook the steaks for 2 minutes on each side for medium-rare and 3 minutes on each side for medium. Meanwhile, preheat the broiler.

Transfer the steaks onto a broiler pan. Mound the Roquefort mixture onto each steak and place under the broiler just long enough to melt the cheese, about 2 minutes. Place on warm serving plates.

Meanwhile, to prepare the salad, peel, core, and slice the pear and toss in a little of the vinaigrette to keep it from turning brown. Mix the watercress, mesclun greens, and pear in a large salad bowl. Add enough vinaigrette to lightly coat the greens (start with ¼ cup and add more if necessary). Garnish the salad with the chopped walnuts. Serve the salad from the bowl or on individual chilled salad plates.

WINE SUGGESTION: *A hearty Burgundy from the northern part of the region is a natural match for steak and Roquefort. The favored regions are Vosne-Romanée, Gevrey-Chambertin, and Chambolle-Musigny. A powerful northern Italian wine, Amarone, would also be a fine choice.*

We have adapted James Beard's original recipe not only by cutting down on the thickness of the steaks but also by reducing the amount of Roquefort called for from 1 cup. If available, consider adding a little escarole or chicory to the salad.

FOR THE STEAKS:

¾ cup Roquefort (about 6 ounces)

2 tablespoons butter

1 tablespoon Worcestershire sauce

2 tablespoons sliced chives

4 strip-sirloin steaks, prime or choice grade, 11 ounces each and about 1½ inches thick

Freshly ground black pepper, to taste

FOR THE WATERCRESS AND MESCLUN SALAD:

1 pear

1 bunch watercress (about 4 ounces), leaves only

3 cups mesclun salad mix

¼ cup walnuts, toasted and coarsely chopped (page 210)

THAI MEATBALLS WITH SPICY PEANUT SAUCE

Serves 4

Everything about this recipe—the flavors, aromas, and combinations of ingredients—will transport you to Southeast Asia, and give you a warm and exotic feeling even if it is fall outside. The delicious peanut sauce works as well with the Skewered Beef Satay (page 80) as it does with these out-of-the-ordinary meatballs.

·······································

To prepare the meatballs, thoroughly combine the beef, ginger, chile, scallion, lemongrass, cilantro, salt, pepper, and sesame oil in a mixing bowl. Divide the mixture evenly into 16 (or 20 smaller) balls. Heat the peanut oil in a sauté pan and cook the meatballs over medium-high heat, turning occasionally until browned on all sides, for 10 minutes (for medium), or to desired doneness.

To prepare the sauce, place the coconut milk, peanut butter, brown sugar, soy sauce, rice vinegar, onion, shallots, garlic, curry paste, lemongrass, lime leaves, cilantro, and basil in a large saucepan. While stirring, bring just to a simmer over medium-low heat; do not boil. Continue to cook, stirring frequently, until the sauce thickens. Turn off the heat, adjust the seasonings, and strain before serving. If you wish a thicker consistency, combine ½ tablespoon of cornstarch with 1 tablespoon of water, stir to dissolve, and mix into the sauce until thoroughly combined; continue to cook until the sauce reaches the desired consistency.

FOR THE MEATBALLS:

1½ pounds lean high-quality ground beef

2 teaspoons finely minced ginger

1 red jalapeño or Fresno chile, seeded and finely minced (about 2 teaspoons)

1½ tablespoons finely minced scallion

½ tablespoon finely minced lemongrass, or ½ teaspoon finely minced lemon zest

1½ tablespoons minced cilantro

½ teaspoon salt

¼ teaspoon pepper

1 teaspoon toasted sesame oil

1 tablespoon peanut, macadamia nut, or vegetable oil

For the Spicy Peanut Sauce:

3 cups unsweetened
   coconut milk
¾ cup smooth peanut
   butter
⅓ cup brown sugar
⅓ cup soy sauce
1½ tablespoons
   unseasoned rice
   vinegar
1 small onion, finely
   diced
2 tablespoons minced
   shallots
2 tablespoons minced
   garlic
¼ cup Thai red curry
   paste
1 tablespoon minced
   lemongrass (about 3
   stalks)
3 kaffir lime leaves (or 1
   teaspoon chopped
   lime zest)
2 cups minced cilantro
¼ cup finely minced basil
½ tablespoon cornstarch
   mixed with 1
   tablespoon water
   (optional)

1 recipe Jasmine Rice
   (page 203) or 1 recipe
   Short-Grain Sticky
   Rice (page 204)

Divide the rice among serving plates, and top with the meatballs and sauce.

Wine Suggestion: *A wine of quality and strength, such as a Chianti Classico from Italy, a Cabernet Sauvignon from the Médoc in Bordeaux, or a Hermitage from the Rhône Valley.*

Sticky rice makes a good substitute for the jasmine rice, but if you prefer, use regular Long-Grain White Rice (page 205). We call for ¼ cup of curry paste in this recipe, but you can reduce this amount or increase it by a tablespoon or so, depending on your heat tolerance.

APPLE BURGERS WITH GERMAN POTATO SALAD

Serves: 4

These burgers, which can also be grilled, are excellent on a cool fall day, or for an end-of-season barbecue to welcome in the fall. The slight sweetness of the apples in the burgers pairs well with the tangy potato salad. This potato salad recipe contains more onion than most, which is good news for onion lovers. For anyone else, the amount of onion can be cut by half.

· ·

To prepare the salad, place the potatoes in a large saucepan of salted water to cover and bring to a boil. Turn down the heat and simmer for 15 to 20 minutes, or until just tender. Drain the potatoes and cut into ¼-inch slices. While the potatoes are cooking, sauté the bacon in a large skillet over medium heat for 3 minutes, or until cooked through. Remove the bacon, chop, and set aside. Add the onions to the pan and sauté for about 7 minutes or until softened. Add the sliced potatoes and toss lightly to coat with the fat. In a bowl, whisk together the vinegar, chicken stock, mustard, and sugar and add to the potatoes. Turn the heat down to low, add the pickle and reserved bacon, and cook the potatoes until most of the liquid is evaporated. Season with the sugar, salt, and pepper. Serve warm or at room temperature.

For the burgers, heat the vegetable oil in a nonstick sauté pan and sauté the shallots over medium heat for about 5 minutes, or until softened. Turn down the heat to medium-low, add the apple, and cook for about 7

For the German Potato Salad:

1½ pounds russet potatoes, peeled

3 slices bacon

2 onions, halved and sliced

½ cup cider vinegar

¼ cup chicken stock, or water

1 tablespoon Dijon mustard

½ teaspoon sugar

¼ cup diced garlic pickle (about 1 spear)

Salt and freshly ground black pepper to taste

1 teaspoon vegetable oil

2 shallots, minced

1 Granny Smith apple,
   peeled and grated

1 tablespoon balsamic
   vinegar

1 pound lean high-
   quality ground beef

¾ teaspoon chopped
   rosemary

1 tablespoon Dijon
   mustard

Salt and freshly ground
   black pepper to taste

1 tablespoon olive oil

4 ounces sharp Cheddar
   cheese, cut into 4
   slices (optional)

2 tablespoons prepared
   mayonnaise

4 large brioche rolls or
   hamburger buns, split
   and toasted

minutes longer, or until softened, stirring occasionally. Stir in the balsamic vinegar and cook until the liquid is evaporated. Remove from the heat and let cool.

In a mixing bowl, thoroughly combine the beef and the apple mixture, rosemary, and mustard. Season with salt and pepper and form into patties. Let rest in the refrigerator for about 30 minutes.

Heat the oil in a large heavy skillet or sauté pan. Sear the burgers over medium-high heat for 1 minute on each side. Turn down the heat to medium and continue to cook for about 3 minutes per side, or until the internal temperature reaches 160 degrees (or medium). About 1 or 2 minutes before the burgers are finished, top with the slices of cheese (if using), cover the pan, and let the cheese melt. Spread some of the mayonnaise on the top half of each roll. Lay the burger on the bottom half. Serve the burger open-faced with a large helping of German Potato Salad on the side.

Wine Suggestion: *A Tavel Rosé from the Rhône Valley is the perfect fit. Alternatively, a French Beaujolais Villages, or Gamay Beaujolais from California.*

Other traditional additions to the potato salad you might consider are chopped celery and diced apple. Start preparing the potato salad about 30 minutes before cooking the burgers. We recommend investing in a good-quality meat thermometer, available from Williams-Sonoma, Omaha Steaks retail stores, or any well-equipped kitchen store. (For the Omaha Steaks retail store nearest you, call 1-800-228-9521, or visit the company's website at www.omahasteaks.com)

SAUERBRATEN WITH POTATO PANCAKES
Serves 4

Sauerbraten is a sweet-and-sour German pot roast. Adding gingersnaps (or *Lebkuchen*) is an optional step to add flavor and help thicken the sauce. *Lebkuchen*, German spiced Christmas cookies, are used in traditional recipes but gingersnaps are less expensive and make a perfectly fine substitute. If you are feeling particularly adventurous, bake some gingerbread cookies and use those.

....

To prepare the marinade, combine the wine, vinegar, onion, carrot, juniper berries, peppercorns, cloves, and bay leaves in a large mixing bowl. Add the beef and refrigerate, covered, for 3 days. Turn the meat at least twice a day.

Remove the meat from the marinade. Strain the marinade, reserving the liquid and discarding the solids. Dry the beef thoroughly.

To prepare the sauce, plump the raisins in the water for 15 minutes. Drain. Heat the olive oil in a Dutch oven or casserole. Sear the beef over medium-high heat for about 10 minutes, until golden brown on all sides. Remove the beef and set aside. Turn down the heat to medium and sauté the onions and carrot for 5 or 6 minutes, or until the onions are golden brown. Add about 1 cup of the reserved marinade to the pan, scraping the bottom to release any drippings. Place the meat on top of the onions and carrot, and cover with the remaining marinade. Bring the marinade to a boil, cover, and turn

For the Marinade and Beef:

2 cups dry red wine

1 cup red wine vinegar

1 onion, diced

1 carrot, diced

6 juniper berries, crushed

1 tablespoon black peppercorns

8 cloves

3 bay leaves

2 pounds top-round beef roast, choice grade

For the Sauce:

½ cup golden raisins

½ cup warm water

2 tablespoons olive oil
   (or bacon fat)

2 onions, chopped

1 carrot, chopped

6 gingersnaps, crushed

Salt and freshly ground
   black pepper to taste

Red wine vinegar, to
   taste

down the heat to low. Simmer as slowly as possible for about 3 hours, or until the meat is fork-tender. Turn the meat once or twice during cooking. About 15 minutes before the meat is ready, add the crushed gingersnaps to the pan. When the meat is tender, remove and keep warm.

With a spoon, remove any fat from the surface of the sauce. Transfer the sauce and vegetables to a food processor and puree. Strain the sauce and return it to the pan, pushing down on any small chunks to break them down. Adjust the seasonings with salt, pepper, and the vinegar. If the sauce is too thick, add a little water to thin. Return the beef to the pan, add the raisins, cover, and simmer for about 10 minutes or until the beef is heated through.

About 45 minutes before you are ready to serve the beef, prepare the pancakes.

Peel and grate the potatoes one at a time and pat dry with paper towels. Transfer to a mixing bowl and toss with the flour and then with the beaten eggs. Season with salt and pepper. In a nonstick skillet, melt ½ tablespoon each of the butter and oil over medium heat. Add the potato mixture to the pan, pressing down to compact it and covering the cooking surface. Fry on one side over medium heat for 4 or 5 minutes, or until golden brown.

Take another skillet of similar size and melt the remaining butter and oil over medium heat. Flip the potato pancake into the prepared pan. Fry for about 3 minutes, then turn down the heat to low and cook for about 20 minutes, or until cooked through. (Alternatively, place in a 400 degree oven, uncovered, and bake for 25 to 30 minutes.) Season with salt and pepper, place on a large heated platter, cut into 4 or 8 slices, and serve immediately.

The beef may be carved in your kitchen or at the table. Arrange the beef on a warm platter, spoon some of the sauce over the top, and garnish with the parsley. Serve the remaining sauce in a sauceboat on the side. Serve with the potato pancake.

WINE SUGGESTION: *The sweet character of the sauerbraten deserves the richness and subtle sweetness of an Italian Amarone; a California Merlot is another excellent choice.*

Flour is often added to the sauce to make a gravy; however, we prefer to thicken the sauce with the vegetables from the braising liquid. Note that the beef should marinate for 3 days.

The potatoes for the pancakes must be peeled right before using or they will turn black. It is important to dry them as much as possible—otherwise you will need to add more flour. When cooking the pancakes, if 2 pans the same size are not available, slide the pancake onto a large platter while adding more oil and butter to the pan; then turn the pancake back into the pan.

FOR THE POTATO PANCAKES:

3 Idaho potatoes (about 1½ pounds)
¼ cup all-purpose flour
2 eggs, beaten
Salt and freshly ground black pepper to taste
1 tablespoon butter
1 tablespoon vegetable oil

2 tablespoons chopped parsley, for garnish

ITALIAN MEATLOAF AND WILD MUSHROOMS BRAISED IN WHITE WINE WITH ASPARAGUS RISOTTO

Serves 4

FOR THE MEATLOAF:

2 tablespoons olive oil

1 onion, diced, plus 1 onion, sliced

2 garlic cloves, minced

2 slices "day old" bread

2 tablespoons milk

1½ pounds lean high-quality ground beef

½ cup freshly grated Parmesan cheese

2 tablespoons chopped prosciutto, or other cured ham

2 eggs, beaten

Salt and freshly ground black pepper to taste

1 tablespoon butter

1 cup dry white wine

½ cup Beef Stock (page 200)

6 ounces wild mushrooms (such as porcini or shiitakes), sliced

2 tablespoons minced parsley

1 tablespoon minced lemon zest

This is a meatloaf dish worthy of being served even on more formal occasions. Traditionally, in Italy, risotto would be offered as a first course, and you may serve it that way if you prefer. When prepared correctly, there is simply nothing that compares to risotto. It is not difficult to do, but the process does require constant attention, and it should always be prepared just before serving as it does not hold well.

••

To prepare the meatloaf, heat 1 tablespoon of the olive oil in a small saucepan and sauté the diced onion over medium heat until golden, about 7 minutes. Add the garlic and sauté an additional 2 or 3 minutes. Remove from the heat and let cool. Pulse the bread in a food processor until crumbs form (you will have about 1 cup of crumbs). Set aside ½ cup for the meatloaf. Spread out the remaining crumbs on a baking sheet to let them dry out until you use them later (if they are still soft when ready to use, place the baking sheet in an oven on low heat for about 10 minutes before using). Mix the ½ cup bread crumbs with the milk and squeeze to release all the liquid you can; discard the liquid. Place the sautéed onion and garlic, dampened bread crumbs, beef, Parmesan, prosciutto, and eggs in a large mixing bowl and mix gently to combine. Season with salt and pepper. Form the mixture into a cylindrical meatloaf (it must be able to fit into a large loaf pan, an oval ovenproof casserole, or a cooking dish with a 10-inch diameter; the meatloaf

12 ounces asparagus

3 cups water

Salt to taste

2 cups vegetable stock, or
    chicken stock

1 teaspoon salt

5 tablespoons butter

2 tablespoons olive oil

2 tablespoons minced
    onion

1½ cups Arborio rice

½ cup freshly grated
    Parmesan cheese

Salt and freshly ground
    black pepper to taste

can also be cooked in a fish poacher). Roll the meatloaf in the reserved dried bread crumbs. Transfer to a platter and let rest in the refrigerator for 30 minutes.

Preheat the oven to 400 degrees.

Heat the remaining tablespoon of oil in a sauté pan and sauté the sliced onion over medium heat for 7 or 8 minutes, until golden. Remove and set aside. Melt the butter in the loaf pan, casserole, or cooking dish, add the meatloaf, and sauté on all sides for 7 or 8 minutes, or until golden brown. Handle the meatloaf gently so that it does not break apart. Add the wine, stock, mushrooms, and sautéed sliced onion, and bring to a simmer. Cover, and transfer to the oven. Braise for about 45 minutes, or until the meatloaf is no longer pink on the inside and the internal temperature reaches 160 degrees. Note that the internal temperature of the meatloaf will continue to rise by 5 to 10 degrees after it has been removed from the oven. Transfer the meatloaf to a heated serving platter. With a spoon, skim any fat from the surface of the sauce. Spoon the sauce with the mushrooms over the meatloaf. Mix the parsley and lemon zest, and sprinkle it over the meatloaf.

While the meatloaf is braising, prepare the risotto. Trim the asparagus, removing any large or woody ends. Place 2 cups of the water and the salt in a saucepan, and bring to a boil. Add the asparagus, turn down the heat to low, and simmer, covered, until just tender, about 7 or 8 minutes (cooking time will be determined by the size of the asparagus; if you are using pencil asparagus, it will take 3 or 4 minutes.) Remove the asparagus, reserving the cooking liquid, and dry on paper towels. Cut the asparagus into ¾-inch lengths, discarding any tough stringy pieces.

Add the cooking liquid to the stock and the remaining 1 cup of water in a clean saucepan and bring to a low simmer. In another heavy saucepan, melt 3 tablespoons of the butter and the 2 tablespoons of oil and sauté the asparagus over medium heat for 2 or 3 minutes; remove and set aside. Add the onion and sauté for 5 minutes longer, or until softened. Add the rice and cook for 2 or 3 minutes, stirring occasionally, until well coated. Turn the heat down to medium-low, stir in about ½ cup of the asparagus broth, and cook until the liquid is almost all absorbed. Add another cup of broth and continue to cook, stirring occasionally to prevent the rice from sticking to the bottom. Repeat this process, adding simmering broth to the rice in small increments until you have used about 4 cups of broth. Then, begin adding the broth about ¼ cup at a time, until the rice is almost cooked (if you run out of broth, add simmering water). Return the asparagus to the pan to warm through. Cut the remaining 2 tablespoons of butter into ½-inch cubes and gently stir into the risotto with the cheese; cook about 2 or 3 minutes before seasoning with salt and pepper. Serve the risotto immediately, with the meatloaf.

WINE SUGGESTION: *A Gattinara from Italy or a Barbera or Petite Syrah from California.*

The amount of broth needed for the risotto will vary depending on how quickly the rice cooks and how much broth is absorbed during cooking; do not hesitate to use more or less as you see fit. When adding the broth to the rice, try to maintain a brisk simmer, so that each addition cooks out fairly quickly, otherwise the rice will become glutinous. You can substitute ¼ cup of white wine for the same amount of broth if you like. The finished risotto should be tender and creamy but still have a bitable texture (that is, *al dente*).

BEEF TOURNEDOS WITH VEGETABLES AND SPINACH IN COCONUT CURRY

Serves 4

FOR THE ROASTED RED POTATOES:

3 tablespoons olive oil

2 garlic cloves, minced

1½ pounds new red potatoes (8 to 12 potatoes, depending on size)

Salt and freshly ground black pepper to taste

FOR THE BEEF:

1½ pounds beef tenderloin
Salt and pepper to taste

2 tablespoons olive oil

12 sprigs cilantro, for garnish

This is one of those delicious dishes with lots of interesting and tantalizing flavors but where no single flavor dominates. When we tested it, it was enjoyed equally well by friends with conservative tastes who don't particularly enjoy anything spicy or exotic, and at the other end of the spectrum, friends who *only* like foods that are spicy and flavorful! There are few dishes that satisfy such diverse groups as these. The potato accompaniment may seem plain, but nothing more is needed with this wonderful aromatic sauce.

Preheat the oven to 400 degrees.

To prepare the potatoes, combine the olive oil and garlic in a mixing bowl. Add the potatoes to the bowl, a few at a time, and rub the garlic oil over the potatoes. Season with salt and pepper. (Larger potatoes can be cut in half or quartered). Arrange the potatoes in a single layer on a baking sheet and roast in the oven for about 35 minutes, or until tender enough to cut with a fork, tossing them occasionally with a little more oil.

Meanwhile, to prepare the vegetable curry, heat the oil in a large saucepan and sauté the onion over medium-high heat for 8 to 10 minutes, until browned. Turn down the heat to medium, add the peppers and jalapeño, and cook for about 5 minutes, until softened. Stir in the garlic and ginger and sauté for 3 or 4 minutes, until fragrant. Stir in the cumin, coriander, and turmeric, and cook for 3 to 4 minutes longer. Add the eggplant and tomatoes, and cook over medium heat, covered, for about 15 minutes or until the eggplant is cooked through, stirring occasionally. Pile the spinach and cilantro on top of the vegetables and cook, covered, for 5 minutes longer, until the spinach has wilted. Remove the lid, stir in the coconut milk, and bring to a simmer. Season with salt and pepper and simmer gently for about 5 minutes, until the sauce is thickened and the consistency of heavy cream.

Slice the tenderloin into 8 equal portions (about 3 ounces each); cut portions from the tapered end of the tenderloin longer and flatten each steak so the tournedos are approximately the same size. Season the tournedos with salt and pepper. Heat the olive oil in a skillet and sauté the tournedos over medium-high heat for about 2 minutes on each side for medium-rare, or 2½ to 3 minutes on each side for medium. Turn down the heat and sauté for 1 minute longer on each side.

To serve, spoon the curried vegetables in the center of warm serving plates. Place 2 tournedos on top of the vegetables and place 2 or 3 potatoes to the side. Garnish each steak with 3 cilantro sprigs and serve immediately.

WINE SUGGESTION: *The abundant spiciness in this dish calls for a more acidic wine, such as a Beaujolais or Italian Bardolino. A Spanish Rioja or a California Gamay Beaujolais, made in a similar style, will also work well.*

This dish can be made equally well with lamb. The vegetables can be prepared earlier in the day up to the point where the coconut milk is added. Then, when ready to serve, reheat the vegetables over low heat and add the coconut milk. If you like picante food, then by all means do not seed the jalapeños, and consider adding a pinch of cayenne at the end.

FOR THE VEGETABLE AND SPINACH CURRY:

1 tablespoon olive oil

1 onion, diced

1 red bell pepper, seeded and diced

1 green bell pepper, seeded and diced

2 jalapeño chiles, seeded and minced

2 tablespoons minced garlic

2 tablespoons minced ginger

1 teaspoon ground cumin

1 teaspoon ground coriander

1 teaspoon ground turmeric

6 ounces eggplant (unpeeled), diced (from a baby eggplant or about ½ medium-sized eggplant)

4 Roma tomatoes, diced

10 ounces spinach leaves, well washed

¼ cup chopped cilantro

1¼ cups unsweetened coconut milk

Salt and freshly ground black pepper to taste

DR. JOHNSON'S STEAK AND OYSTER PUDDING

Serves 4 to 6

FOR THE FILLING:

¼ cup all-purpose flour

Salt and freshly ground black pepper to taste

2 pounds top-round or chuck steak, choice grade, cut into 1-inch cubes

¼ cup butter or olive oil

1 onion, minced

2½ cups sliced mushrooms (about 8 ounces)

½ cup red wine

1½ cups Beef Stock (page 200)

1 tablespoon Worcestershire sauce

1 tablespoon chopped parsley

2 teaspoons chopped marjoram or oregano

This is a traditional English tavern dish that has been served for centuries and can still be found on pub menus today. Reputedly, it was a favorite of the famous eighteenth-century diarist and social commentator Dr. Samuel Johnson. Its heyday was probably in past centuries when oysters were commonplace rather than a luxury. If you like beef pies but dislike oysters, simply omit the seafood.

• •

To prepare the filling, place the flour in a mixing bowl and season with salt and pepper. Dredge the beef in the flour mixture. Heat the butter in a large saucepan, add the beef, and brown in 2 batches over medium-high heat, about 5 minutes. Remove the beef and set aside. Add the onion and mushrooms and cook for 5 minutes, while scraping the drippings from the bottom of the pan. Add the wine, stock, Worcestershire sauce, parsley, and oregano, and gently mix together. Return the beef to the pan, season with salt and pepper, cover, and bring to a boil. Reduce heat to low and simmer for 1½ hours.

Meanwhile, prepare the crust. Place the flour, bread crumbs, and salt in a food processor and pulse to combine. Add the shortening and pulse until the mixture becomes crumbly. Add the water and mix until the dough just comes together in clumps. Cut into 2 pieces; the first should be two-thirds of the total, with the second the remaining one-third. Chill for 30 minutes.

Roll out the larger piece of dough on a lightly floured

work surface to form a circle with a thickness of about $\frac{1}{8}$ inch; the circle should be large enough to fit in the bottom and up the sides of a lightly greased 1-quart baking dish. Press the pastry into the dish, pressing against the sides without stretching the pastry. Trim the edge of the pastry about $\frac{1}{2}$ inch beyond the edge of the dish and add the trimmings to the smaller piece of dough.

Preheat the oven to 350 degrees.

Transfer the beef mixture to the dish and add the oysters. Roll out the remaining piece of dough in a circle to fit the top of the pudding. Trim around the edges of the top piece of pastry and use any extra pastry to make small leaves or flowers, a large *x*, or a design of your choice to decorate the top of the pastry. Moisten the edges of both pieces of pastry with the beaten egg; press and pinch together to seal. Brush the top of the pudding with the remaining beaten egg. Make 3 small holes in the crust to let steam escape. Cover loosely with foil and place in a water bath. Fill the water bath with boiling water, making sure it does not come up further than $\frac{1}{2}$ inch from the rim of the baking dish.

Carefully transfer to the oven and cook for $1\frac{1}{2}$ hours, adding more water to the water bath as necessary. Remove the dish from the water bath, uncover, and continue to bake for 30 minutes or until the crust is a dark golden color.

To serve, remove from the oven and spoon equal portions of the pudding onto warm serving plates. Serve with the mashed potatoes.

WINE SUGGESTION: *A lighter-style red will work here, such as California Merlot or comparable choice from St. Émilion (Bordeaux).*

FOR THE PASTRY CRUST:

2 cups all-purpose flour

$\frac{1}{4}$ cup fresh white bread crumbs

$\frac{1}{4}$ teaspoon salt

$\frac{2}{3}$ cup chilled shortening

$\frac{1}{2}$ cup cold water

8 freshly shucked small oysters

1 egg, beaten

1 recipe Red Chile Mashed Potatoes (page 57)

Cooking the pudding in a water bath helps the crust remain light. To make a truly authentic English-style steak, kidney, and oyster pie, simply add 8 ounces of chopped beef kidney at the same time you add the beef.

CLASSIC ITALIAN MEATBALLS WITH SPAGHETTI

Serves 4

FOR THE MEATBALLS:

1 tablespoon olive oil

1 onion, diced

2 garlic cloves, minced

1 pound lean high-quality ground beef

1 egg, beaten

½ cup fresh bread crumbs

3 tablespoons red wine

¼ cup minced sun-dried tomatoes (packed in oil)

¼ cup freshly grated Parmesan cheese

1 tablespoon chopped oregano

¼ teaspoon dried red pepper flakes

Salt and freshly ground black pepper to taste

½ cup dried bread crumbs (see sidebar, page 143)

2 tablespoons olive oil

2 cups Beef Stock (page 200)

Many people assume that Columbus was Spanish, given the conquests that followed soon after his momentous voyage to the New World, and although he was dispatched by the king of Spain, Chris was in fact Italian—Genoa's best-known son. More than 500 years after his discoveries, his name is still commemorated in the United States every October, and what better way to mark the day than a classic and much loved dish from Columbus's homeland.

• •

To prepare the meatballs, heat the olive oil in a small saucepan and sauté the onion over medium heat until golden, about 5 minutes. Add the garlic and sauté for 2 to 3 minutes longer. Transfer to a mixing bowl and let cool. Add the beef, egg, fresh bread crumbs, wine, tomatoes, cheese, oregano, and red pepper flakes to the bowl, and season with salt and pepper. Gently combine the mixture and let rest for 30 minutes in the refrigerator.

Form the beef mixture into 16 balls and roll them in the dried bread crumbs. Heat the olive oil in a large saucepan over medium heat. Add the meatballs (in batches if necessary) and sauté for 4 or 5 minutes, or until browned on all sides. Remove and set aside. Add the stock and bring to a simmer. Add the meatballs, return to a simmer, cover the pan, and braise the meatballs for 12 to 15 minutes, until no longer pink on the inside.

To prepare the sauce, heat the olive oil in a large

saucepan or stockpot. Add the onion, carrot, and celery, and sauté over medium-low heat for about 10 minutes, or until the onions are translucent and the vegetables are softened. Add the garlic and sauté for 2 minutes longer. Raise the heat to medium, add the chopped tomatoes, wine, and mushrooms, and bring to a simmer. Turn the heat down to medium-low and simmer the sauce for 1 hour, uncovered, to thicken and to allow the flavors to develop (if the sauce begins to get too thick, add up to 1 cup of vegetable stock or water). Stir in the parsley, oregano, and rosemary, and season with salt and pepper. (If the sauce has a slightly bitter taste, add a pinch of sugar.) Add the meatballs and stir gently to mix thoroughly and warm through.

Cook the spaghetti until just tender *(al dente)*, according to package directions. Drain and transfer to warm serving plates. Ladle the meatballs and sauce over the spaghetti.

WINE SUGGESTION: *Almost any Italian red wine is favored here; try a Bardolino, Gattinara, Chianti Classico, or Barbaresco. A Spanish Rioja is also well suited.*

The spaghetti can be cooked in advance, cooled down (by running under cold water), and refrigerated until needed. To reheat, simply drop in boiling water until warm.

The meatballs call for both fresh and dried bread crumbs—the former for internal texture and the latter to make a nice golden coating—but in a pinch, use dried for both.

Almost any fresh herbs can be added to the meatballs and the tomato sauce. Add them near the end of the cooking process so their flavor is not lost. If using dried herbs, add them when you sauté the garlic, so their flavors develop during cooking.

FOR THE TOMATO SAUCE:

¼ cup olive oil

1 onion, diced

1 carrot, diced

1 stalk celery, diced

3 garlic cloves, minced

1 large can (28 ounces) chopped plum tomatoes, with liquid

½ cup dry red wine

4 ounces button mushrooms, sliced (about 1⅓ cups)

2 tablespoons chopped parsley

2 teaspoons chopped oregano

½ teaspoon chopped rosemary

Salt and freshly ground black pepper to taste

12 ounces to 1 pound dried thin spaghetti

PÂTÉ-AND-PASTRY-COVERED BEEF WELLINGTON WITH STUFFED BABY PUMPKINS

Serves 4 to 6

FOR THE BEEF WELLINGTON:

2 tablespoons olive oil

2 pounds prime or choice center-cut beef tenderloin, trimmed

Salt and freshly ground black pepper to taste

2 tablespoons brandy

3 tablespoons butter

8 ounces mushrooms, finely sliced (about 2½ cups)

1 small onion, cut into slivers

1 package (17.3 ounces) frozen puff pastry, thawed

7 ounces chicken liver pâté or foie gras

1 egg, beaten

"Beef Wellington" conjures up images of the famous nineteenth-century English general, the vanquisher of Napoleon, and later, his nation's prime minister. Strangely, references to this dish are hard to find in British cookbooks. However, it seems likely that this technique of encasing beef in pastry, which was popular back then, was named for the national hero. This is a dish for a special occasion, and it makes a fine alternative to the ubiquitous Thanksgiving turkey. The baby pumpkins not only make a unique presentation but can be eaten together with the potato filling.

· ·

Heat the olive oil in a heavy cast-iron skillet. Season the beef with salt and pepper and sear over high heat on all sides, about 5 or 6 minutes (cook for 2 minutes longer if you prefer the beef to be cooked to medium rather than medium-rare). Reduce the heat to medium, carefully pour brandy over the beef, and let it evaporate. Remove the beef from the pan and set aside. Add the butter to the pan and when melted, add the mushrooms and onion. Sauté over medium-high heat for 8 to 10 minutes, until golden, tender, and the pan is almost dry. Remove and set aside.

Place both sheets of the puff pastry on a clean work surface and fold them out. Take the end one-third of one sheet and add it to the end of the other sheet, pinching the edges together to form one long sheet. Arrange the mushrooms and onion carefully down the center of the

1 pound russet potatoes,
    peeled and chopped
2 tablespoons butter
¼ cup milk
½ cup grated Gruyère or
    Jarlsberg cheese
Salt and freshly ground
    black pepper to taste
4 to 6 large baby
    pumpkins, about 8
    ounces each

long sheet of puff pastry. Spread the pâté over the top of the beef and turn the beef over on top of the mushroom mixture so that the pâté is on top of the mushrooms. Fold the puff pastry up and around the beef as far as it will go, and use half of the remaining smaller sheet of pastry to completely enclose the beef in a neat package. Gently pinch the edges of the pastry together where the two sheets join. Form the remaining puff pastry into thin strips and arrange on top in a crisscross lattice design, attaching to the package with beaten egg. Transfer to a baking sheet and brush the surface of the pastry with the remaining beaten egg. Chill in the refrigerator for 30 minutes.

Preheat the oven to 450 degrees.

Meanwhile, to prepare the pumpkins, place the potatoes in a saucepan of salted water to cover, and bring to a boil. Turn down the heat and simmer for 15 to 20 minutes, or until just tender. Drain the potatoes and mash them with a fork or ricer. Add the butter and milk and continue to mash. Add the cheese and season with salt and pepper.

While the potatoes are cooking, cut the tops off the pumpkins, reserving the tops. Scoop out the seeds and strings (a grapefruit spoon works well). Fill a large saucepan with an inch or so of water and bring to a boil. Turn down the heat to low and carefully add the pumpkins; the water should only come halfway up the sides of the pumpkins. Cover the pan with a lid and steam for about 15 minutes, or until tender; place the pumpkin lids on the pumpkins for the last 5 minutes of steaming. Remove the lids and set aside; remove the pumpkins with a slotted spoon and drain upside down on paper towels. Season the insides with salt and pepper, and fill to the top with the mashed potato mixture. Transfer to a baking sheet and set aside.

Bake the Beef Wellington in the oven for 15 minutes. Turn down the heat to 350 degrees and cook for 20 minutes longer or until the pastry is golden brown. Let rest for 15 minutes before serving. While the beef is cooling, bake the pumpkins in the oven for 10 minutes, until warmed through. Then, broil the pumpkins for 5 minutes in a preheated broiler, until the top of the potato is browned and a little crisp. Before serving, place the pumpkin lids a little askew on top of the stuffed pumpkins so the filling shows. Slice the Beef Wellington and serve with the pumpkins.

WINE SUGGESTION: *The best California Cabernet Sauvignon or Grand Cru Classé Bordeaux would complete the winning formula for an exquisite occasion.*

Ask your butcher to trim the fat and silver skin from the tenderloin and make sure the side muscle is removed. Foie gras gives this dish a delicious richness, but you may certainly omit it, or substitute a thin layer of Dijon mustard. If you prefer, you may roll out one sheet of puff pastry to wrap the beef; it will need to be thinner than if you use the two sheets called for in this recipe.

4. RECIPES FOR WINTER

Recipes for Special Occasions

**Red Flannel Corned Beef Hash
with Poached Eggs, page 163**

HUBERT KELLER'S ALSATIAN BAECKEOFFE

Serves 6 to 8

Hubert Keller, who inspired the soup recipe on page 33, is also the author of this wonderful recipe that is a tradition in his native Alsace. In his cookbook *The Cuisine of Hubert Keller* (Ten Speed Press), Hubert explains that in the Alsatian dialect, Baeckeoffe means "baker's oven." Traditionally, the women would prepare this dish on Sunday evening and leave it with the baker to cook in his gradually cooling oven on Monday while they headed down to the river to wash the family's clothes. The baker would seal the casseroles with leftover dough and on the way back with their clean clothes, the women would pick up their casserole and a loaf of bread.

....

Combine the marinade ingredients in a mixing bowl. Add all the meats and toss gently. Cover, and refrigerate overnight.

Preheat the oven to 350 degrees.

Season the potatoes with salt and pepper, and lightly oil a large ovenproof casserole (preferably earthenware and with a vent hole in the lid) with olive oil. Cover the bottom of the casserole with half of the potato slices. Remove the meats and vegetables from the marinade and reserve the marinade. Arrange the mixed meats over the potatoes, and then place the vegetables in a layer over the meats. Cover with a layer of the remaining potato slices and pour the marinade over them. Add enough additional white wine or water to just cover the top of the potatoes. Place the lid on the casserole.

FOR THE MARINADE:

2 onions, minced

2 small leeks, white and tender green parts, julienned

1 carrot, cut into $\frac{1}{8}$-inch slices

3 garlic cloves, finely minced

2 bay leaves

1 teaspoon juniper berries

1 sprig thyme

3 tablespoons finely minced parsley

3 cups dry white wine (preferably Alsatian Riesling)

Salt and freshly ground black pepper to taste

For the Meat:

1 pound beef chuck
roast, choice grade, cut
into 1¼-inch cubes

1 pound boneless pork
butt, trimmed and cut
into 1¼-inch cubes

1 pound boneless lamb
shoulder, choice grade,
trimmed and cut into
1¼-inch cubes

1 pound pigs' feet
(optional)

3 pounds Yukon gold
potatoes (or other
yellow potatoes),
peeled and cut into
⅛-inch-thick slices
Salt and freshly
ground black pepper
to taste

For the Pastry Seal:

¾ cup all-purpose flour
5 tablespoons water
1 tablespoon olive oil
1 egg, beaten (optional)

For the pastry seal, mix together the flour, water, and olive oil in a mixing bowl, and form into a rope shape long enough to wrap around the rim of the casserole. Press the dough onto the rim of the casserole. Place the lid on top of the dough and press to seal completely (this seal will prevent any of the cooking liquid from evaporating). Brush the pastry seal with egg, if a glossier look is desired.

Place the casserole in the oven and cook for about 3 ½ hours. Remove the casserole and bring to the table. Cut under the lid to break the pastry seal and remove the lid. Serve the baeckeoffe out of the casserole onto warm serving plates.

WINE SUGGESTION: *Hubert Keller suggests Alsatian Riesling; Red Bordeaux will also complement the meats in this recipe.*

This is one of only two recipes in this book that uses other meat as well as beef. Note that the meat needs to be marinated overnight. It's a good, easy dish to make for a party and you'll have fun explaining its origin. The casserole must have a vent hole in the lid so the steam can escape while the dish is cooking. Hubert recommends serving this dish with a green salad and a rustic, crusty bread.

CLASSIC LASAGNE WITH MEATBALLS, SAUSAGE, AND RICOTTA

Serves 4 to 6

In Italy, this particular style of lasagne is called *vinci grassi*. Some people prefer a less chunky meat sauce with their lasagne, and if you prefer, you are welcome to substitute your favorite homemade spaghetti sauce for the meatballs and tomato sauce used here. Either way, you can't lose! The white sauce in this recipe is called *besciamella* in Italy, which, as the name suggests, is the equivalent of the classic French béchamel sauce. Serve this dish with crusty garlic bread.

· ·

Heat 1 tablespoon of olive oil in a nonstick sauté pan. Prick the sausages all over with a fork and sauté over medium heat until brown on all sides, about 5 or 6 minutes. Remove and drain on paper towels; when cool enough, cut into slices, chop, and set aside.

In a mixing bowl, combine the ground beef, garlic, onion, bread crumbs, egg yolks, parsley, and oregano. Season with salt and pepper and form into small meatballs, about the size of large olives; there should be about 30 meatballs. Heat the tablespoon of olive oil in the same sauté pan and cook the meatballs over medium-high heat until browned on all sides, about 5 or 6 minutes. Remove, drain on paper towels, and set aside. When cool, cut the meatballs in half.

To prepare the tomato sauce, heat the olive oil in a saucepan, add the garlic and onion, and sauté over medium-high heat for 5 minutes. Add the tomatoes, tomato paste, wine, honey, oregano, dried herbs, and bay

1 tablespoon olive oil
8 ounces spicy Italian
   sausage

FOR THE MEATBALLS:
1 pound lean high-
   quality ground beef
1 garlic clove, minced
½ cup minced onion
¼ cup seasoned bread
   crumbs
2 egg yolks
1 tablespoon minced
   parsley
1 tablespoon minced
   oregano
Salt and freshly ground
   black pepper to taste
1 tablespoon olive oil

For the Tomato Sauce:

1 tablespoon olive oil

2 garlic cloves, minced

1 onion, diced

3½ cups crushed canned tomatoes (28-ounce can), with liquid

¼ cup tomato paste

¼ cup red wine

½ teaspoon honey, or sugar

1 tablespoon minced oregano

2 teaspoons dried mixed herbs, such as Herbes de Provence

2 bay leaves

leaves, stir well, and bring to a boil. Season with salt and pepper, add the sausage and meatballs, reduce the heat to medium-low and simmer, uncovered, for 20 minutes. Remove the bay leaves.

Meanwhile, prepare the white sauce. Place the milk and bay leaf in a small saucepan. Stick 2 cloves in each onion, add to the pan, and bring to a boil. Turn off the heat and let infuse for 20 minutes, uncovered. Strain, discarding the solids. Melt the butter in a separate saucepan and when it begins to bubble, add the flour. Stir together over medium heat to form a thick paste or roux. Gradually stir in the infused milk, bring to a boil, and simmer, stirring frequently, for 5 or 6 minutes. Season with salt, pepper, and nutmeg. Keep warm.

Meanwhile, bring a large saucepan of salted water to a boil and add the lasagne. Cook until just *al dente*, about 10 minutes or according to package directions. Drain and rinse the lasagne in cold water. Spread in a single layer on a wet towel to prevent it from sticking.

Preheat the oven to 350 degrees.

Using a lightly greased 9 by 12-inch baking dish, ladle in half of the white sauce and top with one-third of tomato sauce with meatballs and sausage. Cover with a layer of lasagne noodles, and then all of the ricotta, spreading it out gently and evenly. Cover with one-third of the tomato sauce and another layer of lasagne noodles. Top with the remaining white sauce and finally the remaining tomato sauce. Sprinkle with the Parmesan cheese.

Bake the lasagne in the oven for about 40 minutes, until the top is golden and bubbly (cover with foil if the top browns too quickly). Remove from the oven and let sit for 10 minutes before serving.

WINE SUGGESTION: *A hearty Italian wine such as Chianti Classico or Valpolicella, or a West Coast Pinot Noir.*

If using smaller pans, just keep alternating the various layers until the ingredients are all used up. If you prefer a milder filling, use plain Italian sausage rather than the spicy type.

FOR THE WHITE SAUCE:

3 cups milk

1 bay leaf

4 cloves

2 large pearl onions or boiling onions, peeled

3 tablespoons butter

2 tablespoons sifted all-purpose flour

Salt and freshly ground black pepper to taste

Pinch of nutmeg

FOR THE LASAGNE:

8 ounces dried lasagne noodles

1 pound ricotta cheese

1½ cups freshly grated Parmesan cheese

BIG BEND TEXAS-STYLE CHILI

Serves 4 to 6

The saying goes that there are as many chili recipes in Texas as there are Texans; why, even LBJ, the late president, had his own favorite recipe. There are many schools of thought when it comes to the subject of chili. Some purists favor chopped beef, others ground beef, as here; some swear by kidney beans, others dismiss them as an adulteration! Whatever their preferences, chili fans should know that every fall in Terlingua, a hamlet nestled in the mountainous Big Bend area of southwestern Texas, a national chili cookoff is held that arouses considerable passions. Grizzled old hands and aspiring cooks alike converge on the area from all quarters and enjoy one another's company as well as the world-class chili.

. . . .

To prepare the chili, heat the olive oil in a large saucepan. Add the garlic and onions, and sauté over medium-high heat for 5 minutes. Add the beef and sauté for 7 or 8 minutes longer, while stirring frequently, or until the beef is well browned on all sides. Season with salt and pepper, stir in the chile powder, and cook for 2 minutes more. Add the tomatoes, tomato paste, beef stock, beer, vinegar, cumin, oregano, and parsley, and stir well to combine. Bring to a simmer, turn down the heat to low, and cook, covered, for 45 minutes. Add the beans and cook for 15 minutes longer, stirring occasionally. Ladle into serving bowls and sprinkle with the goat cheese.

WINE SUGGESTION: *Since this dish contains dark beer, consider using the same beer as a beverage. A lighter style of red wine such as a Beaujolais or Italian Bardolino will also work well with these flavors.*

Most chili dishes actually taste better the next day, after the flavors have had time to marinate and marry. You can use black beans instead of kidney beans if you prefer, or a mixture of the two.

2 tablespoons olive oil

5 garlic cloves, minced

2 onions, diced

1½ pounds lean high-quality ground beef

½ teaspoon salt

1 teaspoon freshly ground black pepper

2 tablespoons pure red chile powder

4 Roma tomatoes (about 8 ounces), blanched, peeled, and diced (page 207)

½ cup tomato paste

½ cup Beef Stock (page 200)

1 cup dark beer

2 tablespoons cider vinegar

¾ teaspoon ground cumin

2 teaspoons minced oregano

¼ cup minced parsley

1 can (15 ounces) red kidney beans, drained

4 ounces crumbled goat cheese, for garnish

FOR THE CURRY:

1¼ pounds strip sirloin,
choice grade, cut into
1-inch cubes

½ cup plain yogurt

3 garlic cloves, minced

1 tablespoon minced
ginger, or 1 teaspoon
ground dried ginger

½ tablespoon ground
coriander

½ tablespoon ground
cumin

½ tablespoon ground
garam masala
(optional)

½ tablespoon pure red
chile powder

1 tablespoon finely
chopped (or ground)
almonds

Salt to taste

2 tablespoons peanut oil

1 onion, diced

1 can (14 ounces)
crushed tomatoes,
with liquid

2 tablespoons freshly

This recipe is a family tradition that has been passed down through the generations by a good friend of ours. There are countless types of curry on the Indian subcontinent; those from the north of India are quite different in style from those found in the south, which often contain coconut or tamarind, or in Bengal to the east or Gujarat to the west. This recipe contains elements found in the traditional *pasanda* meat curry and *korma gosht*, a similar type of meat curry in a rich sauce. The flavorful lentil dish is called *dal* in Indian cuisine.

To prepare the curry, place the meat, yogurt, garlic, ginger, coriander, cumin, garam masala, chile powder, chopped almonds, and salt in a mixing bowl. Combine thoroughly, cover, and let marinate in the refrigerator for at least 1 hour. Heat the peanut oil in a saucepan and sauté the onion over medium-high heat for 7 or 8 minutes, or until golden. Add the meat mixture and cook for about 10 minutes, or until well browned, stirring frequently. Add the tomatoes, lemon juice, and 1 tablespoon of the cilantro, and cook for 45 minutes longer, until the meat is tender, stirring occasionally. Just before serving, garnish with the remaining tablespoon of cilantro and the slivered almonds.

While the curry is cooking, prepare the lentils. Place the lentils and water in a saucepan and add the turmeric and coriander. Bring to a boil, turn down the heat, and simmer for about 30 minutes, or until just tender. Add a

squeezed lemon juice

2 tablespoons chopped
  cilantro

4 teaspoons slivered
  almonds, for garnish

FOR THE LENTILS:

1 cup yellow or red
  lentils, rinsed

2 cups water

½ teaspoon ground
  turmeric

1 tablespoon ground
  coriander

1 jalapeño chile, seeded
  and minced

1 cup canned crushed
  tomatoes

5 curry leaves (optional)

Salt to taste

½ tablespoon clarified
  butter (optional)

1 tablespoon minced
  onion (optional)

1 tablespoon chopped
  cilantro, for garnish

FOR THE RICE:

1½ cups basmati rice

4 cups cold water

½ teaspoon salt

½ teaspoon freshly
  squeezed lemon juice

little more water if necessary to keep moist. Let cool slightly and then transfer half of the mixture to a blender and puree. Lightly mash the remaining lentils in the pan and return the pureed lentils to the pan. Stir in the chile, tomatoes, and curry leaves, and season with salt. Cover the pan and cook over low heat for 30 minutes. Just before serving, heat the clarified butter in a small skillet and add the onion. Sauté over medium heat until golden brown and pour over the lentils. Garnish with the cilantro.

Meanwhile, place the rice in a saucepan and add the water and salt. Let sit for 20 minutes so the rice can soak. Bring to a boil, add the lemon juice, and cover the pan. Turn the heat down to low and simmer for about 15 minutes, or until the water is absorbed and the rice is tender. Do not stir the rice while it is cooking.

To serve, spoon the rice on one side of warm serving plates and ladle the curry on top of the rice. Serve with the lentils next to the rice.

WINE SUGGESTION: *A Spanish red will balance the intense flavors of this recipe; alternatively, consider a white wine, such as a California Sauvignon Blanc, or a fruity Alsatian Gewürztraminer.*

This recipe calls for individual spices—you are in effect making your own curry powder blend. We think this makes an interesting alternative to using a prepared curry powder, and you can adapt the proportions to suit your own palate; this recipe makes a fairly mild curry, so for more heat, increase the amount of chile powder. These spices, and the curry leaves, are available from Indian markets or gourmet food stores. However, if you have trouble finding them, or if you prefer, use a ready-made blend. For a further shortcut, simply omit the *dal*—you will still have a delicious and filling meal.

CLASSIC POT AU FEU
Serves 6

This classic French boiled beef dish (which translates as "pot on fire") is simple to prepare and yields a double dividend: the cooking broth is served as a soup for the first course, while the cooked beef and vegetables form the main course. In France, this popular dish arouses considerable passions and every year, pot au feu festivals are held across the country. A good pot au feu cannot be rushed: allow at least 4 hours for the brisket to cook. Serve the soup with good crusty bread, and as optional garnishes, offer cornichons, pickled onions, mustard, and horseradish.

•••

Place the beef and salt pork in a stockpot and add the stock and water (add more of each if necessary to cover the beef). Place the bay leaves, cloves, peppercorns, thyme, parsley, and marjoram in a piece of cheesecloth and secure. Add this *bouquet garni* to the pot, add the salt, and cover the pot. Bring to a boil over medium heat, skimming off any impurities that rise to the surface with a large spoon. Add the carrots, celery, parsnips, turnip, onion, leeks, and garlic, and simmer, covered, for 3½ hours, skimming the surface occasionally. Add the potatoes. Wrap the marrow bones in cheesecloth, add to the pot, and simmer for 30 minutes longer or until the beef is tender.

Remove the beef, transfer to a serving platter, and slice. Serve the cooking liquid as a first-course soup. Remove the *bouquet garni* and the wrapped marrow

3 pounds beef brisket, with fat point removed, or eye of round, cut in half crosswise (across the grain), choice grade

1 pound salt pork, quartered

4 cups Beef Stock (page 200)

8 cups water

2 bay leaves

5 cloves

2 teaspoons black peppercorns

3 sprigs thyme

3 sprigs parsley

3 sprigs marjoram

2 teaspoons salt

5 carrots, sliced on the diagonal about ¼ inch thick (about 2 cups)

(continued)

1 stalk celery, sliced on
   the diagonal about ¼
   inch thick (about 1
   cup)
2 parsnips, peeled and
   diced (about 1 cup)
1 cup diced turnip
1 cup chopped onion
5 leeks, white and light
   green parts, sliced
3 garlic cloves
2 pounds white or red
   potatoes, peeled and
   diced
3 small beef marrow
   bones (optional)

bones. For the entree, place the sliced beef on warm
serving plates with the cooked vegetables.

WINE SUGGESTION: *A robust West Coast Pinot Noir or a
French Burgundy will balance the richness of this dish.*

Cooking the marrow bones in cheesecloth, like the *bouquet garni*, prevents the contents from escaping. Some guests will enjoy scooping out the marrow with a small spoon, so offer them that option; if they accept, serve the marrow bones with toast so they can spread the marrow and enjoy the contrasting textures. Other vegetables you may add or substitute are fennel bulbs (quartered); celery root (quartered); cabbage (cut into wedges); and fava beans.

RED FLANNEL CORNED BEEF HASH WITH POACHED EGGS

Serves 8

Corning beef was an important method of preserving beef in the days before refrigeration, and ranked with smoking and drying as common techniques. It's probably not time- and effort-efficient to prepare homemade corned beef just for this recipe—it takes 8 to 12 days to cure—but if you are so inclined, then sources such as *The New York Times Cookbook* contain recipes for corning beef. Red flannel hash is a traditional New England embellishment of corned beef hash, and is so called because of the addition of the beets. It makes a wonderful brunch dish.

....

To prepare the hash, melt the butter in a sauté pan or skillet and sauté the onion and bell peppers over medium-high heat for 5 minutes. Transfer to a mixing bowl and add the corned beef, beets, egg, Worcestershire sauce, pepper, and nutmeg. Mix thoroughly and let rest in the refrigerator for at least 4 hours or overnight.

Heat the olive oil in a sauté pan, add the potatoes, and sauté over medium-high heat for 8 to 10 minutes, or until golden brown, stirring frequently. Set aside.

Heat ½ tablespoon of the vegetable oil in each of 2 large sauté pans. Add one quarter of the hash mixture to each pan and cook over medium heat for about 2 minutes. Add the sautéed potatoes and continue cooking for 6 to 8 minutes or until crispy, shaking and flipping the pan or stirring frequently with a spatula. Remove and keep warm while repeating for the remaining hash mixture.

FOR THE HASH:

2 tablespoons butter
1 onion, finely diced
¼ cup finely diced red bell pepper
¼ cup finely diced green bell pepper
1 pound good-quality corned beef, finely diced
2 cups diced cooked beets (2 or 3 beets, weighing about 1 pound)
1 egg, lightly beaten
1 teaspoon Worcestershire sauce
Freshly ground black pepper to taste
¼ teaspoon ground nutmeg
½ tablespoon olive oil
1½ pounds russet potatoes, peeled and diced
2 tablespoons vegetable oil

To prepare the eggs, bring a medium saucepan of salted water to a boil and add the vinegar. Break 4 eggs, one at a time, into a saucer and then slip carefully into the pan. Cook until the egg whites are set and firm, about 4 minutes. Remove with a slotted spoon and let drain. Repeat for the remaining 4 eggs. To serve, place the hash on warm serving plates, top with a poached egg, and garnish with freshly ground black pepper.

WINE SUGGESTION: *Gamay Beaujolais from California or a Tavel Rosé from France.*

> While this recipe calls for poaching the eggs, you can fry them to the desired doneness instead, or even loosely scramble them.

FOR THE EGGS:
8 eggs
2 tablespoons white wine vinegar
Freshly ground black pepper, for garnish

SZECHUAN HOT-FRIED CRISPY SHREDDED BEEF WITH CARROTS

Serves 4

Szechuan is the largest province of China, and its cuisine has a reputation for spiciness and bold, pungent flavors. The food in this landlocked, western region through which the headwaters of the Yangtze River flow is not for wimps! Beef is more common here than in other parts of the country, and it is typically "dry-fried," as in this recipe, with little liquid added.

••

Prepare the rice.

Meanwhile, place the eggs in a shallow bowl, add the beef, and coat thoroughly. Add 1 tablespoon of the sherry, the cornstarch, and the salt, and mix the ingredients so the beef is well coated. Heat the sesame oil and peanut oil in a wok over high heat. When just smoking, add the beef and 1 tablespoon more of the sherry and stir-fry over high heat for 3 or 4 minutes, until the beef is browned and no longer sticks together. Turn down the heat to medium and continue to stir-fry for 2 minutes longer.

Add the garlic, ginger, bean paste, soy sauce, hot chile sauce, hoisin sauce, sugar, and the remaining 2 tablespoons of sherry, and stir-fry for 1 minute. Increase the heat to high again and add the carrots, bell pepper, and celery. Stir-fry for 2 minutes. Add the scallions and pepper, stir together well, and serve over the rice.

WINE SUGGESTION: *A very full-bodied, rich wine is needed here, such as Hungarian Egri Bikavér (Bull's Blood), Chilean Cabernet, or Italian Barbera. A hearty California Zinfandel will also match successfully.*

> Ideally, the beef, carrots, and celery should be julienned into strips about the size of matchsticks. For best results, freeze the beef for 30 minutes before cutting it. The beef and egg mixture may seem a little "clumpy" when you begin cooking it, but it will soon separate and "dry-fry."

1 recipe Long-Grain White Rice (page 205)

2 eggs, beaten

1 pound top sirloin, cut into thin strips 1 inch long and $\frac{1}{8}$ inch thick

4 tablespoons sherry

2 tablespoons cornstarch

$\frac{1}{4}$ teaspoon salt

2 tablespoons toasted sesame oil

2 tablespoons peanut oil

2 garlic cloves, minced

2 tablespoons minced ginger

1 tablespoon black bean paste

$\frac{1}{2}$ tablespoon soy sauce

1 teaspoon hot chile sauce

1 tablespoon hoisin sauce

1 tablespoon sugar

3 carrots, julienned

1 small red bell pepper, seeded and julienned

1 stalk celery, julienned

$\frac{1}{4}$ cup sliced scallions

$\frac{1}{4}$ teaspoon freshly ground Szechuan pepper (optional)

BEEF AND GUINNESS PIE WITH MUSHROOMS AND CHESTNUTS

Serves 4

¼ cup olive oil

1 ½ pounds beef top round, choice grade, cut into 1-inch cubes

4 slices bacon, chopped

1 large onion, diced

1 garlic clove, minced

2 carrots, sliced

1 stalk celery, sliced

8 ounces mushrooms, stemmed and quartered

2 tablespoons all-purpose flour

1 cup Beef Stock (page 200)

1 cup Guinness

1 cup peeled and roasted chestnuts (page 209)

Salt and freshly ground black pepper to taste

Pastry Crust (page 140)

1 egg, beaten

Mashed Potatoes (page 202)

Slow-cooking beef in a braising liquid of beer is a classic combination that works wonderfully well, as this recipe and the one on page 170 prove. The dark, toasty quality of the black Irish Guinness stout beer is complemented by the roasted chestnuts, smoked bacon, and earthy mushrooms; these ingredients would not match as well with an amber or even a dark red beer, for example.

· ·

Heat the olive oil in a large skillet until hot. Add the beef and bacon, and sear over medium-high heat for about 5 minutes, or until browned on all sides. Add the onion, garlic, carrots, celery, and mushrooms, and cook for 7 or 8 minutes, until the ingredients are soft, stirring occasionally. Sprinkle in the flour and cook for 1 minute before stirring in the stock, Guinness, and chestnuts. Season with salt and pepper. Turn down the heat to low and simmer, covered, for 2 hours, stirring occasionally.

Preheat the oven to 375 degrees. Lightly grease a 1-quart baking dish.

Meanwhile, prepare the pastry crust and line the prepared baking dish with it. Add the filling and roll out the remaining dough to form the top of the pie. Moisten the edges of the top and bottom pieces of pastry with the beaten egg, and press and pinch together to seal. Brush the top of the pie with the remaining beaten egg. Using a sharp knife, cut a few slits in the pastry to make air vents. Place the baking dish in the oven and bake for 45 minutes, or until the top of the crust is golden brown.

While the pie is baking, prepare the mashed potatoes. Remove the pie from the oven and cut into equal portions. Transfer to warm serving plates and serve with the mashed potatoes.

WINE SUGGESTION: *If you choose not to drink Guinness stout with this dish, try a wine with some complexity and power, such as Cabernet Sauvignon from California or a French Bordeaux.*

If you have ever been within sniffing distance of a Guinness brewery (as we have, in West London), you'll recognize the unmistakable aroma captured in the complex and intense flavors of this very different pie.

BRISKET BRAISED IN BEER AND MUSTARD WITH WARM MUSTARD SLAW

Serves 4

FOR THE BRISKET:

3 pounds boneless beef
   brisket, fat point
   removed, choice grade

1 teaspoon freshly
   ground black pepper,
   or to taste

2 tablespoons olive oil

1 cup Beef Stock (page
   200)

1 cup dark beer

1 onion, sliced

2 garlic cloves, chopped

2 tablespoons Dijon
   mustard

2 tablespoons spicy
   brown mustard

¼ teaspoon cayenne

In America, brisket is perhaps most often associated with corned beef or barbecue. Here is another take on this popular cut. This dish can be carved at the table or sliced and used for hearty sandwiches. Serve with rye bread and plenty of chilled beer—preferably the same one used in the braising liquid. Come to think of it, this is an ideal meal for those weekend winter afternoons spent sitting around watching football and drinking beer. So here's another reason to look forward to the playoffs!

•••

Preheat the oven to 300 degrees. Season the brisket with the pepper. Heat the olive oil in a Dutch oven or ovenproof casserole and sear each side of the brisket over medium heat until browned on all sides, about 6 minutes. Add the stock, beer, onion, garlic, Dijon and brown mustards, and cayenne, and bring to a simmer. Cover, and transfer the Dutch oven to the oven. Braise for about 4 ½ hours, or until tender enough to pull apart with a fork (the cooking time will vary depending on the thickness of the brisket); turn the brisket over a few times during cooking if it is not totally immersed in the liquid. Remove the meat and keep warm. Skim the braising liquid to remove any fat and drippings that have been released from the meat. When ready to serve, trim the fat off the brisket, slice the meat, and spoon some of the braising liquid over the slices.

While the brisket is braising, prepare the slaw. Sauté the bacon in a large saucepan over medium heat until all the fat is released, about 3 minutes. Remove the bacon, chop, and set aside. Pour off and reserve all but about 2 tablespoons of the bacon fat in the pan. Add the chicken stock and vinegar, bring to a boil over medium-high heat, and reduce by half. Turn down the heat to medium-low, add the cabbage, and cook for about 3 minutes, until slightly wilted but still crisp. In a cup, combine the heavy cream and mustard and add to the cabbage, stirring to incorporate. Season with salt and pepper and cook for 2 or 3 minutes longer, or until thickened. Heat about 2 teaspoons of the reserved bacon fat in a small saucepan (if there is not enough, use olive oil). Add the mustard seeds and cook over medium heat for 2 or 3 minutes, or until they begin to pop. Pour over the slaw, garnish with the bacon, and serve warm or at room temperature with the brisket and braising sauce.

WINE SUGGESTION: *Since this recipe calls for dark beer, consider the same beer as a beverage. Alternatively, a West Coast Pinot Noir or a Cabernet Sauvignon from California will harmonize well with this dish.*

FOR THE MUSTARD SLAW:

3 slices bacon

½ cup chicken stock

¼ cup cider vinegar

10 ounces red cabbage, thinly sliced

10 ounces green cabbage, thinly sliced

¼ cup heavy cream

4 teaspoons Dijon mustard

Salt and freshly ground black pepper to taste

½ teaspoon mustard seeds

While braising, the brisket should be at a low simmer; if it is too bubbly, turn down the heat to 275 or even 250 degrees; some ovens run hotter than others. As an option, serve with sweet potatoes that are rubbed with olive oil, cayenne, salt, pepper, and then roasted, or use this combination the next day with any leftover brisket.

MOM'S MEATLOAF WITH ROASTED TOMATO COULIS AND ROASTED GARLIC MASHED POTATOES

Serves 4

FOR THE ROASTED TOMATO COULIS:

8 Roma tomatoes, cored and cut in half lengthwise

1 onion, cut in half

1 jalapeño chile, cut in half lengthwise and seeded

1 head garlic

¾ cup vegetable stock

2 tablespoons extra-virgin olive oil

2 tablespoons chopped parsley

1 teaspoon chopped oregano

¼ teaspoon chopped rosemary

½ teaspoon chopped thyme

Salt and freshly ground black pepper to taste

This dish is delicious comfort food, but with an elegant twist or two. In this recipe, although we do not pour the sauce over the meat when cooking, you can prepare it that way if you (or your guests) prefer. Instead, we like the idea of preparing the meatloaf with the bacon on top—picking the bacon off before eating the meatloaf seems like such a treat. Bear in mind that the shape of the loaf will determine the exact baking time; you can reduce the baking time by forming the meatloaf into 4 individual loaves.

• •

Preheat the oven to 350 degrees. To prepare the coulis, place the tomatoes, onion, and jalapeño cut side down on an oiled baking sheet, add the whole head of garlic, and roast in the oven about 1 hour, or until the tomatoes begin to blacken and the onion is soft. Remove 4 garlic cloves from the head of garlic and squeeze out the pulp; reserve the remaining roasted garlic for the mashed potatoes. Puree the tomatoes, onion, jalapeño, and squeezed garlic pulp in a food processor or blender for 2 or 3 minutes, or until smooth, adding about ¼ cup of the stock if necessary to make pureeing easier. Heat the olive oil in a saucepan, add the pureed vegetables, remaining vegetable stock, parsley, oregano, rosemary, and thyme, and cook over medium heat until reduced slightly and thick enough to coat the back of a spoon, about 20 minutes. Season with salt and pepper. Reheat the coulis just before serving.

Preheat the oven to 350 degrees. To prepare the meatloaf, soak the bread crumbs in the milk, and then squeeze out and discard the liquid. Heat the olive oil in a small saucepan and sauté the onion over medium heat until softened, about 5 minutes. Add the garlic and sauté for 2 to 3 minutes longer. Transfer to a large mixing bowl and let cool. Add the bread crumbs, bell pepper, beef, eggs, barbecue sauce, ketchup, Worcestershire sauce, parsley, oregano, rosemary, and pepper flakes, and season with salt and pepper. Mix gently to combine but do not overwork the meat, as it will become tough. Form the mixture into a loaf and place on an oiled baking sheet. Cover the top of the meatloaf with the bacon slices and bake in the oven for about 1 hour, or until the meatloaf is no longer pink inside and the internal temperature reaches 160 degrees. Note that the internal temperature of the meatloaf will continue to rise by 5 to 10 degrees after it has been removed from the oven.

About 30 minutes before serving, prepare the mashed potatoes. Squeeze the roasted garlic from 8 of the reserved cloves and mash into the potatoes. Season the potatoes with salt and pepper to taste, and serve immediately.

To serve, carefully transfer the meatloaf to a warm serving platter. Spoon the warm coulis around the meatloaf and serve the mashed potatoes on the side.

WINE SUGGESTION: *A powerful wine with body, such as an Italian Amarone, Chianti Classico, or a French Châteauneuf-du-Pape.*

The oil in the coulis can be omitted although it provides rich flavor. If you double the amount of coulis (to yield about 4 cups), you can serve it alone for a meal with penne or bowtie pasta (you might want to keep the amount of stock the same while doubling all the other ingredients). This recipe calls for keeping the blackened skin on the tomatoes and jalapeño, but remove it if you prefer.

FOR THE MEATLOAF:

1 cup fresh bread crumbs

¼ cup milk

1 tablespoon olive oil

1 onion, diced

2 garlic cloves, minced

1 red bell pepper, roasted, peeled, seeded, and diced (page 207)

1½ pounds lean high-quality ground beef

2 eggs, beaten

½ cup prepared barbecue sauce

¼ cup tomato ketchup

2 teaspoons Worcestershire sauce

¼ cup chopped parsley

1 tablespoon chopped oregano

1 teaspoon chopped rosemary

1 teaspoon dried red pepper flakes

Salt and freshly ground black pepper to taste

6 slices bacon

1 recipe Mashed Potatoes (page 202)

MARINATED LONDON BROIL WITH STEWED PINK BEANS AND PUMPKIN

Serves 4

For the Achiote Oil:

¼ cup achiote seeds

½ cup vegetable oil

For the Marinade and Beef:

3 garlic cloves, mashed to a paste

1 teaspoon dried oregano

1 teaspoon ground cumin

1 teaspoon salt

½ teaspoon freshly ground black pepper

½ teaspoon dried red pepper flakes

1½ pounds top-sirloin London broil, approximately 1¼ inch thick, prime or choice grade, cut from the cap

The vegetable component of this dish (in contrast to the name of the cut of beef) is adapted from a traditional Puerto Rican bean stew. Ask your butcher for top-sirloin London broil; sometimes, London broil is cut from flank steak, which makes an acceptable alternative. In Puerto Rico, this dish is usually served with white rice that has been steamed until a crust forms on the bottom of the pan. Salt pork is often used in Puerto Rican cooking, and you can substitute it for the bacon in this recipe.

· ·

To prepare the oil, pick through the achiote seeds to remove any sediment. Heat the vegetable oil in a small saucepan over medium heat. Add the seeds and cook for 2 or 3 minutes, or until they just begin to pop and the oil turns golden red. Strain the oil into a clean container. It can be held in the refrigerator for several weeks.

For the marinade, in a mixing bowl, combine ¼ cup of the achiote oil with the garlic, oregano, cumin, salt, pepper, and red pepper flakes. Spread over both sides of the London broil and refrigerate for 2 hours.

Rinse the drained beans under cold running water and transfer to a saucepan, covering with 2 to 3 inches of water. Bring to a boil, turn down the heat to a simmer, and cook for 1½ to 2 hours, or until just tender, skimming the surface occasionally to remove any impurities. When the beans are cooked, pour off and discard all but about

1 cup of the cooking liquid. Reserve the liquid separately from the beans. Set aside.

Heat 1 tablespoon of the achiote oil in a large saucepan over medium heat and sauté the bacon until the fat is released, about 3 minutes. Remove the bacon, chop, and set aside. Add the onions to the pan and sauté for about 5 minutes, or until softened. Add the garlic and cook for 2 to 3 minutes longer. Add the bell pepper and cubanelle pepper and cook for about 5 minutes, or until softened. Add the tomatoes, oregano, and cilantro, and cook for 3 or 4 minutes longer, until the mixture is fairly dry. Transfer this mixture to the beans, add the pumpkin, bacon, and the reserved cup of cooking liquid, and stir to incorporate. Bring to a boil over medium-high heat. Turn down the heat and simmer the beans, covered, for 15 to 20 minutes or until the pumpkin is tender but not falling apart. Season with salt and pepper to taste; add water if the stew gets too thick.

While the beans are cooking, preheat the broiler.

Place the London broil in a large roasting pan and broil for 4 to 5 minutes on each side for medium-rare, about 5 or 6 minutes per side for medium, or to the desired doneness. Before serving, carve into ¼-inch slices.

Serve the beans in large bowls alongside the beef.

WINE SUGGESTION: *A wine with a higher acidity works best here, such as a Spanish Rioja or Italian Bardolino.*

FOR THE STEWED PINK BEANS AND PUMPKIN:

8 ounces dried pink beans or pinto beans, soaked overnight and drained

2 slices bacon

2 onions, chopped

2 garlic cloves, minced

1 green bell pepper, seeded and chopped

1 cubanelle pepper or green Italian pepperoncino, chopped

3 tomatoes, blanched, peeled, seeded, diced (page 207)

2 teaspoons chopped oregano

2 tablespoons chopped cilantro

8 ounces pumpkin, peeled, seeded, and cut into 1-inch cubes

Salt and freshly ground black pepper to taste

Pumpkin is available in Spanish markets year around. If it is not available, use another winter squash, such as butternut or acorn. Achiote (or annatto) seeds were used by early Amazon tribes to paint their bodies as well as to season and color foods. They remain a key ingredient in many Caribbean and Latin American dishes. In the United States, achiote is used primarily to color cheeses, butter, and margarine; it can be found in most Spanish markets. As an alternative, use 2 tablespoons of paprika.

BEEF ESTERHÁZY WITH CHANTERELLES AND KASHA PILAF

Serves 4

For the Beef Esterházy:

4 top-round steaks, choice grade, about 8 ounces each and ¾ inch thick

2 teaspoons paprika

Salt and freshly ground black pepper to taste

3 tablespoons olive oil

2 onions, sliced

3 carrots, sliced into rounds

4 Roma tomatoes, diced

2 bay leaves

2 cups Beef Stock (page 200)

6 ounces chanterelle mushrooms, trimmed

¼ cup heavy cream

½ teaspoon freshly squeezed lemon juice

Here is another Hungarian classic—a straightforward warming winter dish with similarities to goulash and Swiss steak. In this recipe, we have paired the beef with another Eastern European classic, kasha (roasted buckwheat groats). The buckwheat is steamed in a manner similar to rice and adds a nutty flavor and texture to the dish. If you prefer, noodles or root vegetables may be served instead.

• •

To prepare the Esterházy, pat the steaks dry and rub them with the paprika. Season with salt and pepper and pound the steaks with the flat side of a meat cleaver or a rolling pin for about 30 seconds, just to ensure that the seasoning adheres.

Preheat the oven to 325 degrees. Heat 2 tablespoons of the olive oil in a Dutch oven or large casserole dish over medium-high heat and brown the steaks for 2 minutes on each side. Remove and set aside. Reduce the heat to medium, add the remaining tablespoon of oil to the pan, add the onions and carrots, and sauté for about 7 minutes, or until golden brown. Add the tomatoes and cook for 2 or 3 minutes longer. Place the steaks on top of the vegetables and add any juices that have been released from the meat. Add the bay leaves and stock, and bring to a simmer. Transfer to the oven and braise, covered, for about 1½ hours. Add the mushrooms and continue to braise for 30 minutes longer, or until the steaks are tender enough to be pulled apart with a fork.

Remove the steaks from the casserole and keep warm. Discard the bay leaves and skim any fat from the surface. Stir in the heavy cream and lemon juice, and return just to a simmer on top of the stove; take care not to boil.

Prepare the kasha about 40 minutes before serving. Heat the butter in a sauté pan over medium heat and sauté the onion for about 5 minutes, or until softened. Add the garlic and sauté for 2 minutes longer. Add the mushrooms and cook for about 5 minutes, or until the mushrooms are soft and have released most of their juice. Set aside.

Place the egg in a mixing bowl, add the kasha, and stir until all of the kasha is coated with the egg. Heat a large nonstick saucepan over medium-high heat, add the kasha, and toast for 2 or 3 minutes, stirring constantly, until the grains are separated and the egg is cooked. Turn down the heat to medium-low and add the stock and the reserved cooked onions, garlic, and mushrooms. Season with salt and pepper and cook at a slow simmer, covered, for about 8 minutes, or until all the liquid has been absorbed and the kasha is just tender. Let sit, covered, for about 10 minutes before fluffing with a fork. Stir in the parsley and adjust the seasonings.

Spoon the kasha onto warm serving plates. Place the steaks on the kasha and spoon the sauce and mushrooms over the steaks.

WINE SUGGESTION: *A fine Cabernet Sauvignon from California or red Bordeaux from France.*

We use coarse cracked roasted kasha in this recipe, but whole roasted groats (hulled, crushed kasha) can be prepared the same way—they will just take a little longer to cook.

FOR THE KASHA PILAF:
2 tablespoons butter
½ onion, diced
2 garlic cloves, minced
2 ounces chanterelle or button mushrooms, diced (about ⅔ cup)
1 egg, lightly beaten
1 cup coarsely cracked roasted kasha (buckwheat groats)
2 cups boiling chicken stock
Salt and freshly ground black pepper to taste
2 tablespoons minced parsley

NEW ENGLAND BOILED DINNER WITH HORSERADISH CREAM

Serves 4

FOR THE NEW ENGLAND BOILED DINNER:

3 pounds corned beef brisket

10 black peppercorns

3 cloves

1 bay leaf

6 russet potatoes (about 2 pounds), peeled and cut in half

6 onions, peeled

4 carrots, sliced into 2-inch lengths

4 parsnips, sliced into 2-inch lengths

1 rutabaga, cut into quarters

½ head green cabbage, cut into quarters

Salt and freshly ground black pepper to taste

This is a classic cold-weather "one-pot" supper perfect for family and friends. You can easily stretch this to feed more by adding extra vegetables. This dish cools off very quickly once plated, so if it can't be served immediately, use an ovenproof platter and place it in a low oven. Better yet, the trimmed (but not sliced) meat and vegetables could be held in the stock until ready to serve. Extra corned beef and vegetables can be held with some of the stock in the refrigerator for another meal, or slice the beef and use it for corned beef sandwiches.

••

To prepare the boiled dinner, place the corned beef, peppercorns, cloves, and bay leaf in a large stockpot, cover with cold water, and bring to a boil over high heat. Turn down the heat to low and simmer, covered, for about 3 hours, or until tender. Add the potatoes, onions, carrots, parsnips, and rutabaga, and simmer for 30 minutes longer. Add the cabbage and simmer for 15 to 20 minutes or until cooked through but still firm. Taste the vegetables and add salt and pepper as necessary.

Meanwhile, prepare the horseradish cream. Combine the horseradish, lemon juice, sugar, and salt in a small bowl. Just before serving, whip the cream to soft peaks in a large chilled mixing bowl. Fold in the horseradish mixture. Note that the horseradish cream will not hold well, prepare as close to serving time as possible.

Remove the beef from the pot, carve away all the fat, and slice into ¼-inch-thick slices. Transfer the sliced meat to a large warm serving platter. Remove the bay leaf. Place the vegetables all around the meat, spoon a small amount of broth over the meat and vegetables (just enough to moisten), and serve immediately, with the horseradish cream on the side.

WINE SUGGESTION: *A zesty West Coast Pinot Noir or French Beaujolais Villages makes the right statement for this entree.*

FOR THE HORSERADISH CREAM:

½ cup prepared
   horseradish, drained
1 teaspoon freshly
   squeezed lemon juice
½ teaspoon sugar
¼ teaspoon salt
½ cup heavy cream

The amount of water needed for the boiled dinner will be determined by the size of the pan you choose. You want to cover the corned beef and have enough water so that when the vegetables are added they also will be completely submerged; 2 inches of water above the brisket will do it. If it turns out you need more, simply add simmering water to the pan before the vegetables go in.

The cooking times for the vegetables are estimates and will give very soft—but not mushy—vegetables (except for the cabbage, which we prefer slightly crunchy). If you prefer all your vegetables less tender, add them closer to the end of the cooking, about 30 minutes before you are ready to serve. The horseradish cream adds a touch of elegance to this homey meal, but prepared horseradish, horseradish mayonnaise, or prepared mustard can be served instead.

BEEF AND TOMATILLO TAMALE CASSEROLE WITH ARUGULA SALAD AND LIME VINAIGRETTE

Serves 4 to 6

FOR THE LIME VINAIGRETTE:

¼ cup freshly squeezed lime juice

2 tablespoons white wine vinegar

1 garlic clove, minced

1 tablespoon grated lime zest

2 tablespoons minced cilantro

2 tablespoons olive oil

¼ cup vegetable oil

Salt and freshly ground black pepper to taste

FOR THE ARUGULA SALAD:

12 ounces arugula, washed and stemmed

4 radishes, finely sliced

3 carrots, julienned

2 tomatoes, diced

This Southwestern-influenced casserole is sometimes called tamale pie, but there is really nothing pie-like about it, and the corn base is closer to polenta and grits than tamales. Many people shy away from experimenting with tomatillos, which look like small green tomatoes (the two are not related), but they are wonderful in this recipe; in fact, this is a great recipe for anyone who hasn't used tomatillos before. The casserole can be made 1 or 2 days in advance before baking.

To prepare the casserole, season the beef with 1 tablespoon of the cumin, the salt and pepper, and rub the oil over the beef. Let sit for 30 minutes.

Combine the Cheddar and Monterey Jack cheeses in a bowl and set aside. Puree the tomatillos, onion, and garlic in a food processor for about 4 minutes; the texture should still be somewhat coarse. Heat a large skillet over medium heat and toast the corn for about 7 minutes or until browned, stirring constantly. Turn down the heat to low, add the pureed tomatillo mixture with the sugar and the remaining cumin, and simmer for about 15 minutes, or until thickened. Remove from the heat and stir in the beans, chipotle chile, cilantro, and ¾ cup of the mixed cheeses. Season with salt and pepper and set aside.

Heat a skillet and sear the beef over high heat for 1 to 2 minutes on each side, until browned. Remove and let cool; the beef will be quite rare. Slice the beef across the grain ¼ inch thick, and then cut each slice into strips about 1½ inches long.

Preheat the oven to 400 degrees. In a large saucepan, bring the water and salt to a boil. Slowly add the cornmeal to the water, whisking constantly. Turn down the heat and simmer for 4 or 5 minutes, until thickened. Remove from the heat and stir in ¾ cup of the reserved cheeses. Grease a 9 by 13-inch baking pan and spread half of the cornmeal mixture over the bottom. Spread the vegetable filling over the cornmeal. Lay out the strips of sirloin over the vegetables. Spread the remaining cornmeal mixture over the top, to within 1 inch of the edge (leaving a 1-inch border of vegetables). Sprinkle the remaining cheese around the edge of the pan. Bake the casserole for about 30 minutes, or until the surface is golden and the casserole is bubbling.

While the casserole is baking, prepare the salad dressing. Combine the lime juice, vinegar, garlic, lime zest, and cilantro in a small bowl. Whisk in both oils and season to taste with salt and pepper. Combine the arugula, radishes, carrots, and tomatoes in a large salad bowl. Add half the vinaigrette and toss to combine thoroughly. Add more vinaigrette as necessary or serve on the side.

WINE SUGGESTION: *A light red wine from Spain or a California Gamay Beaujolais will match the tangy flavors of this dish.*

Although we have used top sirloin, any leftover cooked beef can be sliced or shredded and added. Cooked ground beef or even pork or chicken can be substituted. Add leftover cooked vegetables (especially grilled or roasted). To add a completely different flavor, substitute eggplant for the tomatillo.

FOR THE BEEF AND TOMATILLO TAMALE CASSEROLE:

1 pound top-sirloin steak, prime or choice grade, 1 inch thick

1 tablespoon plus 1 teaspoon ground cumin

Salt and freshly ground black pepper to taste

1 tablespoon olive oil

1 cup grated sharp Cheddar cheese

1 cup grated Monterey Jack cheese

1¼ pounds tomatillos, husks removed, rinsed, cored, and quartered (about 8 large tomatillos)

1 onion, quartered

3 garlic cloves, crushed

3 cups frozen corn, thawed (or fresh)

1 teaspoon sugar

2 cups cooked black beans

2 tablespoons minced canned chipotle chile

2 tablespoons chopped cilantro

5 cups water

1½ teaspoons salt

1⅔ cups yellow stone-ground cornmeal

BEEF STROGANOFF WITH BRANDIED MUSHROOMS

Serves 4

1½ pounds completely trimmed beef tenderloin, or tenderloin tips, choice grade

FOR THE MARINADE:
1 onion, thinly sliced
1 carrot, thinly sliced
2 garlic cloves, sliced
2 sprigs thyme
2 bay leaves
Salt and freshly ground black pepper to taste
2 cups dry white wine, or as needed

In our previous book, *The Steaklover's Companion*, we included a recipe for Stroganoff, but here's another recipe with a different twist. Stroganoff dates from eighteenth-century Russia. It is often thickened with roux; however, we have thickened ours with heavy cream to add a richness that the tenderloin deserves. Marinating the meat is not necessary, but it adds a complexity of flavors to the dish.

• •

Slice the beef into ¼-inch by 2-inch slices. Combine the onion, carrot, garlic, thyme, bay leaves, salt, pepper, and tenderloin in a nonreactive bowl and add enough white wine to cover. Marinate, covered, in the refrigerator for 3 or 4 hours. Remove the meat from the marinade and discard the marinade. Dry the beef on paper towels.

Slice the mushrooms in half (or into quarters, depending on their size). Melt the butter in a large sauté pan over medium heat. Add the mushrooms and sauté for about 5 minutes, until softened. Season with salt and pepper, and pour the brandy over the mushrooms. Carefully ignite; when the flames have died down, cover and keep warm.

For the sauce, combine the beef stock and white wine in a saucepan over high heat and reduce by half, about 7 or 8 minutes; set aside. Heat the butter in the large sauté pan and sauté the onion over medium heat for about 7 minutes, or until golden. Add the reduced stock and bring to a simmer. Add the heavy cream and cook at a low simmer for about 5 or 6 minutes, or until the sauce has thickened enough to coat the back of a spoon.

Heat the olive oil and butter in a large sauté pan over medium-high heat. Add the reserved beef and sauté quickly for 3 or 4 minutes until just browned (you may want to do this in 2 batches, so as not to crowd the pan). With a slotted spoon, remove the meat and add it to the sauce. Stir in the sour cream and mustard, and season with salt and pepper; add more mustard if desired. Just before serving, bring the Stroganoff to a simmer again, just enough to warm thoroughly.

About 20 minutes before serving, prepare the egg noodles according to the package directions.

To serve, arrange the egg noodles on 4 warmed serving plates and spoon the Stroganoff on top. Using a slotted spoon, place some of the mushrooms on top of the Stroganoff.

WINE SUGGESTION: *A good-quality Pinot Noir from the West Coast, or a fine Burgundy from France.*

> Tenderloin tips or sirloin can be used instead of the tenderloin, and even leftover tender cooked beef. Small button mushrooms work best in this recipe—they give a more attractive presentation than cut mushrooms.

FOR THE MUSHROOMS:
6 ounces button
    mushrooms
2 tablespoons butter
Salt and freshly ground
    black pepper to taste
¼ cup brandy

FOR THE SAUCE:
1 cup Beef Stock (page
    200)
1 cup dry white wine
1 tablespoon butter
1 onion, finely sliced
¾ cup heavy cream

1 tablespoon olive oil
1 tablespoon butter
¼ cup sour cream
2 teaspoons Dijon
    mustard
Salt and freshly ground
    black pepper to taste

1 pound wide egg
    noodles

MOROCCAN BEEF AND VEGETABLE COUSCOUS WITH HARISSA

Serves 4 to 6

For the Harissa:

3 dried small hot red
chile peppers (such as
arbol), stemmed

½ cup finely ground
walnuts

5 tablespoons extra-
virgin olive oil

2 garlic cloves

1 tablespoon Tabasco
sauce

In northern Africa, couscous (granular semolina) is rolled by hand into small balls and steamed over simmering stew in an earthenware pot called a *couscoussière*. The couscous is then spread on a platter and the stew is ladled over the top. Guests eat from the platter, using crusty bread to sop up the stew. Truly, this is a simple recipe; the most labor-intensive part is cutting the vegetables. Our version uses the commonly available quick-cooking couscous and diners may eat from their own plates, while still helping themselves to the stew, which is placed in the center of the table. Even if you choose to use silverware, we still recommend serving a crisp French baguette on the side.

• •

To prepare the harissa, combine all the ingredients in a blender and blend to a paste. If necessary, add a little water to thin.

To prepare the stew, heat the oil in a Dutch oven over medium-high heat. Add the beef and sear for about 8 minutes, or until golden brown. Turn down the heat to medium, add the onion, and cook for about 5 minutes, until it begins to soften. Add the garlic, half of the tomatoes, the black pepper and red pepper flakes, the cumin, coriander, and cinnamon, and cook for about 5 minutes longer. In a small bowl, mix the saffron in ½ cup of the warm water, soften for 2 or 3 minutes, and add to the meat. Add the remaining 3 cups of water and bring the broth to a boil. Turn down the heat and slowly simmer,

FOR THE STEW:

2 tablespoons olive oil

1 pound choice grade
beef tenderloin tips,
or top sirloin, cut into
1-inch chunks

1 large onion (about 8
ounces), coarsely
chopped

3 garlic cloves, minced

4 Roma tomatoes,
coarsely chopped

½ teaspoon freshly
ground black pepper

½ teaspoon dried red
pepper flakes

½ tablespoon cumin
seeds, toasted and
ground (page 209)

½ tablespoon coriander
seeds, toasted and
ground (page 209)

1 (about 2 inches) length
of cinnamon stick

1 teaspoon crushed
saffron

3½ cups warm water

3 cups water

covered, for about 10 minutes. Skim the surface of the broth to remove any impurities. Add the carrots and simmer, covered, about 5 minutes. Add the potato, squash, and zucchini, and simmer, covered, for 5 minutes longer. Add the eggplant and chickpeas, and simmer, covered, for 5 more minutes. Stir in the remaining tomatoes, the cilantro, and parsley. Season to taste with salt and pepper and simmer, covered, for about 10 minutes longer, or until all the vegetables are tender.

About 20 minutes before serving, prepare the couscous. Bring the water to a boil in a saucepan. Remove from the heat, stir in the couscous, and cover. Let rest for about 10 minutes. Fluff with a fork and season with salt.

To serve, place a heaping pile of couscous on warm serving plates. Spoon a small amount of the stew over the center of the couscous. Fill separate tureens or serving bowls with the remaining couscous and stew, and place them in the center of the table. Put the harissa in a small bowl to pass at the table. Guests may help themselves to the stew and add the harissa to season their meal to taste.

WINE SUGGESTION: *A full-bodied wine such as a Rhône Valley Hermitage or Côte Rôtie, or a powerful Zinfandel from California.*

Harissa, a traditional accompaniment in many North African countries, is a highly seasoned puree that is passed around the table. Diners take a small (or large) amount and stir it into the stew to season it to their liking. James Beard created his own version, adding walnuts (an unusual ingredient) to enrich the hot sauce. We have doubled his original recipe, because we feel certain you will like this so much, you won't want to run out.

2 carrots (about 6 ounces), cut into 1½-inch lengths (larger ends should be split)

1 russet potato (about 8 ounces), peeled and cut into 1½-inch chunks

1 small butternut squash (about 12 ounces), peeled, seeded, and cut into 1½-inch chunks

1 zucchini (about 4 ounces), cut into 1-inch lengths

1 small eggplant (about 8 ounces), cut into 1½-inch chunks

½ cup cooked chickpeas (garbanzo beans)

⅓ cup chopped cilantro (including stems)

⅓ cup chopped parsley

Salt and freshly ground black pepper to taste

FOR THE COUSCOUS:
2 cups water
2 cups couscous
Salt to taste

"GRETNA GREEN" BEEF AND VEGETABLE BROTH WITH WHITE BEANS

Serves 4

For the White Beans:

12 ounces dried white
    beans, soaked
    overnight and drained
2 quarts water

This recipe is named after the town that lies on the border of Scotland and England that was unique (and infamous) for its "quickie" weddings. So why the name of this recipe, you ask? Because this soup takes a nod to the ever-popular Scotch broth, which traditionally is made with lamb. Think of this soup as a wedding between that classic and a hearty bean soup.

•••

Rinse the beans and place in a large saucepan with the water; add more if necessary to keep the beans covered by at least 2 inches. Over medium heat, bring the beans to a boil. Turn down the heat and simmer for 1½ to 2 hours, or until just tender. Remove from the heat, drain, and set aside.

While the beans are cooking, prepare the broth. Put the beef, 1 of the onions, 2 of the carrots, 2 stalks of celery, and 2 cloves of garlic in a large saucepan. Slice 1 of the turnips and add to the pan. Add the water, stock, salt, and peppercorns. Bring to a boil and turn down the heat to low. Cover the pan and simmer for 3 hours. Let cool, skim off any fat, and strain into a clean saucepan; reserve the meat and discard the vegetables. To the saucepan add the remaining onion, carrot, celery stalk, 2 cloves of garlic, the leek, and the pearl barley. Slice the remaining turnip and cut the slices into quarters before adding to the saucepan. Bring to a boil, turn down to a simmer, and cook for 30 minutes. Cut the beef into small chunks (or shred the brisket), add to the saucepan along with the cooked beans, and cook for 10 minutes longer. Serve in large warm serving bowls.

WINE SUGGESTION: *A Beaujolais Villages, a Beaujolais from a specific village such as Fleurie or Juliénas, or a West Coast Pinot Noir.*

> This soup can be made without beans (like Scotch broth), or with different beans.

FOR THE BROTH:

1½ pounds top round, choice grade, or the flat lean part of a boneless beef brisket, choice grade

2 red onions, peeled and finely sliced

3 carrots, peeled and finely sliced

3 stalks celery, finely sliced

4 garlic cloves, finely sliced

2 turnips, peeled

8 cups water

2 cups Beef Stock (page 200)

Salt to taste

10 black peppercorns

1 leek, finely sliced

¼ cup pearl barley

BONELESS RIB-EYE ROAST, ROASTED ACORN SQUASH, AND BUTTERED BRUSSELS SPROUTS WITH CHESTNUTS

Serves 4

FOR THE RIB-EYE ROAST:

2 tablespoons olive oil

4 pounds boneless rib-eye roast, prime or choice grade

Salt and freshly ground black pepper to taste

FOR THE ACORN SQUASH:

2 acorn squashes, cut in half and seeded

1 teaspoon ground ginger

2 teaspoons brown sugar

Salt and freshly ground black pepper to taste

2 tablespoons butter

Is there anything more evocative to meat lovers than the aroma of roasting beef? It definitely adds to the cozy ambiance when the family is gathered together in the house at Christmastime to celebrate and to share. There are two schools of thought when it comes to roasting: quick roasting, and slow roasting. In general, quick roasting is best for prime cuts such as this one (and the standing rib roast on page 42),

while slow roasting is better for less tender cuts, such as shoulder or round. Sprouts and chestnuts are traditional foods for Christmas and the holiday season, and we serve them together in this seasonal recipe.

1 pound brussels
    sprouts, trimmed and
    outer leaves removed
2 cups water
12 to 16 chestnuts,
    roasted and peeled
    (page 209)
¼ cup butter
¼ teaspoon ground
    nutmeg
Salt and freshly ground
    white pepper to taste

Preheat the oven to 450 degrees.

To prepare the roast, heat the olive oil in a heavy skillet over high heat. Sear the beef on each side, about 3 to 4 minutes. Season with salt and pepper. Transfer to a roasting pan and roast in the oven for 10 minutes. Turn down the heat to 375 degrees, baste with the drippings, and roast for 1 ½ hours for medium-rare to medium, or to the desired doneness. Remove from the oven and let rest on a carving board for 5 minutes before slicing.

Prepare the acorn squashes about 45 minutes before you are ready to serve. Sprinkle the flesh of the acorn squashes with the ginger, sugar, salt, pepper, and butter. Place flesh side up on a baking sheet and bake in the oven (with the beef) for about 40 minutes, or until tender.

To prepare the brussels sprouts, make an *x* with a sharp knife on the stem ends and place in a vegetable basket or metal colander set over a saucepan of boiling water. Cover the pan and steam for 8 to 10 minutes or until just tender. Drain and return to the warm pan (off the heat) to dry. Heat the 2 cups of water in a small saucepan and warm the chestnuts through. Drain and add to the sprouts. Transfer to a serving dish and add the butter, nutmeg, salt, and pepper. Toss together gently to coat the sprouts.

Serve the sliced rib-eye roast with the squash, and the sprouts with chestnuts.

WINE SUGGESTION: *This elegant Christmas dinner requires an equally elegant wine. We suggest a fine Cabernet Sauvignon from California or an equally great French Bordeaux.*

BEEF FILET EN CROÛTE WITH GREEN BEANS AND WALNUTS
Serves 4

FOR THE CABERNET REDUCTION:

1 bottle Cabernet Sauvignon wine

FOR THE BEEF EN CROÛTE:

4 filet mignons, about 6 ounces each, completely trimmed, 1¼ inches thick, choice grade

Salt and freshly ground black pepper to taste

2 tablespoons olive oil

3 onions, sliced

3 tablespoons Beef Stock (page 200), or water

1½ teaspoons minced thyme

6 ounces fresh goat cheese

1 sheet puff pastry, 9 inches square (thawed if using frozen)

2 eggs, beaten

This elegant entree makes a fine way to bring in the New Year and it is surprisingly simple to prepare. It can be prepared several hours in advance but should be served immediately after baking. The whole beef filet could be covered by the puff pastry to form one long roll, like Beef Wellington (page 144), but the individual packages called for here make an attractive and simple alternative presentation.

• •

Pour the wine into a small heavy saucepan and bring to a boil. Turn down the heat to low and simmer for 45 minutes to 1 hour, or until ½ cup remains and the consistency is syrupy.

Season the steaks with salt and pepper. Heat 1 tablespoon of the olive oil in a nonstick pan set over medium heat and sear the fillets on all sides, about 1 minute per side, or until browned. Remove the filets and any juices they have released and set aside.

Add the remaining 1 tablespoon of olive oil to the pan and sauté the onions for 5 or 6 minutes or until light golden brown. Turn down the heat to medium-low, add the beef stock and any reserved beef juices, and continue to cook until the onions have cooked all the way through and are moist but not wet, about 5 minutes longer. Stir in the thyme and season with salt and pepper. Transfer to a mixing bowl and let the onions cool completely. Crumble the goat cheese into the onions and mix gently with a fork to incorporate.

FOR THE GREEN BEANS
AND WALNUTS:
1 pound green beans,
   trimmed
1 lemon
2 tablespoons butter
Salt and freshly ground
   black pepper to taste
½ cup walnuts, toasted
   and chopped (page
   210)

Roll out the puff pastry until it measures 14 inches square and then cut into four 7-inch squares (the squares should be large enough to fold around the fillets). Brush the edges of the puff pastry with the beaten egg and place 3 tablespoons of the onion-goat cheese mixture in the center of each square, spreading it out with the back of a spoon. Place the beef filets on top of the mixture and spoon the remaining onion mixture on top of the filets and around the sides. To finish, bring up the 4 corners, and tightly enclose the puff pastry by closing the sides over and using more beaten egg to seal. (Don't worry too much about how this looks as the joined edges will be on the bottom of the puff pastry package when serving.) Turn over the puff pastry and place on a lightly oiled baking sheet. Let rest in the refrigerator for about 30 minutes.

Preheat the oven to 400 degrees.

When ready to bake, remove the packages from the refrigerator and brush the surface with the beaten egg. Bake in the oven for about 20 minutes for medium-rare, 25 minutes for medium, or until the pastry is golden brown. (If the pastry gets browned too quickly, cover with foil and continue to bake.)

About 15 minutes before you are ready to serve, prepare the green beans. Blanch the beans in a saucepan of salted boiling water to cover for about 5 minutes, until they turn bright green and are just tender; they should still have a bite to them. Drain the beans and lay out on paper towels to dry. Zest the lemon with a zester or vegetable grater and set aside. Juice the lemon. Melt the butter in a large skillet over medium heat, add the blanched beans, and sauté for 3 or 4 minutes, taking care not to overcook them. Add the lemon zest, 2 tablespoons of the lemon juice, and season with salt and pepper. Taste, and add more lemon juice if desired. Toss the walnuts with the green beans.

Place the pastry-covered steaks in the center of warmed serving plates. Using tongs, arrange the green beans next to the pastry. Drizzle any remaining butter from the pan over the green beans. Spoon 2 tablespoons of the warmed Cabernet reduction next to the steaks.

WINE SUGGESTION: *Ringing in the New Year with this recipe demands a powerful and elegant wine, such as a fine California Cabernet Sauvignon or a classified Red Bordeaux from France.*

Use small pastry cutters or a sharp knife to cut out decorative shapes from any extra puff pastry and attach to the top of the pastry with beaten egg before baking. Using frozen puff pastry is certainly easier than making puff pastry from scratch, but feel free to use homemade if you prefer. Typically, frozen puff pastry comes 2 sheets to a box, with each sheet measuring 9 inches square, as we have used here.

CHÂTEAUBRIAND FOR TWO WITH LOBSTER TAILS, CHÂTEAU POTATOES, AND BÉARNAISE SAUCE

Serves 2

This is the perfect romantic dinner because Châteaubriand, invented by the chef of the nineteenth-century French author François Châteaubriand, is classically prepared for two. Traditionally, Châteaubriand is served with béarnaise sauce and Château potatoes. Preparing the potatoes may seem like a lot of work, but this is a special meal for a special occasion, and well worth the extra effort.

....

Cut the potatoes into pieces about ¾ inch wide by ¾ inch deep and 1 inch long. Carve each piece into the shape of an olive (relatively uniform pieces will cook evenly). Melt the butter over medium-low heat in a large nonstick sauté pan. Add the potatoes and sauté for about 15 minutes, or until light golden brown and cooked through. Season with salt and pepper, and toss with the parsley. Keep warm.

To prepare the béarnaise, combine the vinegar, wine, shallots, 2 teaspoons of the tarragon, and peppercorns in a small saucepan and bring to a boil. Lower the heat to a simmer and reduce the liquid by half. Let cool until lukewarm. Transfer to the top of a double boiler set over briskly simmering water, and add the egg yolks and lemon juice, whisking constantly until the mixture thickens to the consistency of heavy cream. Add the butter and whisk until the sauce thickens again. Season with salt and pepper and strain the sauce into a clean saucepan; thin with a little water if necessary. Keep

FOR THE CHÂTEAU POTATOES:

1 pound russet potatoes, peeled
2 tablespoons butter
Salt and freshly ground black pepper to taste
2 teaspoons minced parsley

For the Béarnaise Sauce:

2 tablespoons white wine vinegar

1 tablespoon dry white wine

1 tablespoon minced shallots

1 tablespoon minced tarragon

3 black peppercorns, cracked

2 egg yolks

½ teaspoon freshly squeezed lemon juice

½ cup melted butter

Salt and freshly ground black pepper to taste

½ teaspoon minced chervil (optional)

warm, and just before serving, stir in the remaining tarragon and the chervil.

Preheat the broiler. For the Châteaubriand, season the steak with salt and pepper, and place in a shallow bowl. Combine 1 tablespoon of the olive oil with the garlic and spread over the entire steak. Heat the remaining 1 tablespoon of olive oil in a cast-iron skillet over medium-high heat. Sear the steak on all sides for 4 or 5 minutes, or until browned. Transfer to the lowest rack of the broiler and broil for about 10 minutes. Turn the steak and broil for about 10 minutes longer for medium-rare or 12 minutes longer for medium. Remove from the broiler and let rest about 5 minutes before cutting.

Remove the shell from the lobster tail meat and season the lobster with salt and pepper. Combine the butter and garlic and spread on the lobster meat. Place the lobster on a broiler pan and broil on the lowest rack of the broiler for 6 to 8 minutes, or until the lobster is just cooked through.

To serve, spoon about 2 tablespoons of béarnaise sauce onto the center of warm dinner plates and spread out to make a 3-inch circle. Cut the Châteaubriand in half and place it cut side down onto the béarnaise sauce. Place the lobster beside the Châteaubriand so that it curls around the steak. Arrange the potatoes on the other side of the steak. Spoon more béarnaise sauce over the steak and along the length of the lobster. Drizzle extra béarnaise around the edge of the plate, if desired.

This combination of lobster and Châteaubriand presents some interesting wine possibilities. Our first choice, given the special occasion, is a great Champagne from France or a sparkling wine from California. If you are looking for wines to match the food, try either a Sauvignon Blanc from California or a Pouilly Fumé from the Loire Valley in France. If you prefer red wine, choose a West Coast Pinot Noir or a French Burgundy.

Châteaubriand steak is cut from the center of the tenderloin. It is usually cut to about 1¼ pounds, but we suggest a smaller cut, since we are including lobster tails for our special occasion menu. If possible, ask for 12 ounces to 1 pound of center-cut tenderloin. Tarragon vinegar can be substituted for the fresh tarragon in the béarnaise sauce.

FOR THE CHÂTEAUBRIAND:

1 pound center-cut beef tenderloin, prime or choice grade, side muscle removed

Salt and freshly ground black pepper to taste

2 tablespoons olive oil

2 garlic cloves, mashed to a paste

2 frozen lobster tails, about 8 ounces each, thawed

2 tablespoons butter, softened

2 garlic cloves, mashed to a paste

APPENDIX
Basic Recipes and Techniques

**Opposite page: Grilled Porterhouse steak with
Tomato Charlotte, page 76**

BEEF STOCK

Yields about 2 quarts (8 cups)

2 pounds beef bones,
    meat, and trimmings

3 carrots, chopped

2 small onions, chopped

2 cups hot water

1 leek, chopped

1 stalk celery, coarsely
    chopped

2 tomatoes, quartered (or
    1 cup canned plum
    tomatoes, with liquid)

3 garlic cloves, crushed

8 sprigs fresh parsley

2 bay leaves

4 sprigs fresh thyme, or
    ½ teaspoon dried
    thyme

2 tablespoons
    champagne vinegar or
    white wine vinegar

This flavorful stock can be adapted to make veal or lamb stock by simply substituting veal or lamb bones and meat for the beef.

Preheat the oven to 450 degrees.

Place the beef bones, meat, and trimmings in a roasting pan with the carrots and onions. Roast in the oven for 30 to 40 minutes, stirring occasionally, until the mixture is browned. Transfer to a stockpot. Pour off the fat from the roasting pan and deglaze with the hot water, scraping the sides and bottom of the pan to loosen all the pieces. Add this mixture to the stockpot along with the remaining stock ingredients. Add enough water to cover the mixture by 2 inches and bring to a boil. Reduce the heat and simmer the stock for at least 4 hours, uncovered. Occasionally skim off any impurities that rise to the surface as it cooks. Add more water as necessary to keep the mixture covered. Strain, discard the solids, and let the stock cool. Cover and refrigerate until needed (keeps up to 5 days in the refrigerator or can be frozen up to 3 months).

MARK MILLER'S BLACK BEANS

Yield: About 4 cups

Add the barbecue sauce for spicy Southwestern-style beans, but leave it out if you want beans without the smoky flavor.

••

Place the cumin, coriander, oregano, and marjoram in a dry heavy skillet and toast over low heat for about 1 minute, until fragrant, stirring frequently (do not scorch or the mixture will become bitter-tasting). Transfer to a large saucepan and add the beans, onion, garlic, serranos, bay leaves, and tomato puree (add enough water to cover the beans by 2 to 3 inches). Bring the beans to a simmer over medium heat. Cook at a low simmer for about 2 hours, or until the beans are just tender. Add more water if necessary to keep the beans covered as they cook. Season with salt, stir in the barbecue sauce, and continue cooking the beans for about 10 minutes, or until almost all of the liquid has been absorbed. Remove the bay leaves.

1 teaspoon ground cumin

1 teaspoon ground coriander

1 teaspoon dried oregano, ground to a powder in a spice mill or a clean coffee grinder

1 teaspoon dried marjoram, ground to a powder in a spice mill or clean coffee grinder

2 cups dried black beans, picked through and rinsed

1 onion, finely diced

3 garlic cloves, minced

2 serrano chiles, seeded and minced

2 bay leaves

1 cup tomato puree

1 tablespoon salt

1 cup barbecue sauce, preferably a smoky-flavored sauce (optional)

MASHED POTATOES

Yield: Serves 4

1½ pounds potatoes,
   peeled and chopped
2 tablespoons butter
1 cup milk
Salt to taste

As an option, if you enjoy the flavor, add 2 cloves of pureed or roasted garlic while mashing the potatoes.

....

Place the potatoes in a saucepan of salted water and bring to a boil. Turn down the heat and simmer for about 20 minutes, or until tender. Drain and transfer to a mixing bowl. Meanwhile, in a sauté pan, melt the butter with the milk, and bring to a boil. With an electric mixer (or a wire whisk), whip the potatoes while drizzling in the milk mixture as needed. Season with salt.

JASMINE RICE

Yield: About 2 cups

Jasmine rice is an aromatic, delicately scented long-grain rice native to Thailand but now grown in California (Lundberg Family Farms brand, available at many natural foods markets and supermarkets, is excellent).

1 cup jasmine rice
1½ cups water
1 tablespoon butter
Salt to taste

Place the rice, water, butter, and salt in a saucepan with a tight-fitting lid. Bring to a boil, and turn down the heat to a simmer. Cook, covered, for 20 minutes or until the rice has absorbed all the liquid (add a little more water if the rice is not yet tender). Remove from the heat and let stand for 5 minutes. Fluff with a fork before serving.

SHORT-GRAIN STICKY RICE

Yield: 4 to 5 cups

2 cups short-grain rice
2 cups cold water

Also known as Japanese rice because it is favored in that country, sticky rice is more starchy and more glutinous than long-grain rice. Calrose short-grain rice is a commonly available brand.

· ·

Wash the rice several times in cold water. Rinse and drain until the water runs fairly clear. Place the rice in a heavy saucepan and cover with the water. Bring to a boil over medium-high heat, turn down the heat to low, and cover the pan. Steam the rice for 15 minutes; do not remove the lid while the rice is cooking. Turn off the heat and let the rice sit for another 10 minutes before removing the lid. Fluff with a fork and transfer to an attractive covered bowl or individual rice bowls to serve.

LONG-GRAIN WHITE RICE
Yield: About 3 cups

This is a multi-purpose rice recipe. For Indian cuisine, substitute fragrant long-grain basmati (or the domestic Texmati) rice. For Southeast Asian recipes, substitute jasmine rice where appropriate.

1 cup rice
2½ cups water
Pinch of salt

••

Place the rice, water, and salt in a saucepan with a tight-fitting lid. Bring to a boil, and turn down the heat to a simmer. Stir once and cook, covered, for 15 to 20 minutes or until the rice has absorbed all the liquid. Remove from the heat and let stand for 5 minutes. Fluff with a fork before serving.

ROASTING GARLIC

Roasting garlic gives it a sweet, mellow flavor. Place unpeeled garlic cloves in a heavy skillet and dry-roast over low heat for about 30 minutes, shaking or stirring the skillet occasionally, until the garlic becomes soft. Alternatively, place the garlic cloves in a roasting pan and roast in a preheated oven at 350 degrees for 25 to 30 minutes (cooking at 300 degrees for 45 minutes to 1 hour makes the garlic sweeter yet). When the garlic has roasted, peel the cloves, or squeeze the garlic pulp out of the skin.

If you have a toaster oven, use it to roast garlic cloves—it's more energy-efficient.

BLANCHING TOMATOES

Blanching makes tomatoes very easy to peel, and in certain dishes it is advantageous to remove the relatively tough outer skin. Blanching also keeps the texture intact.

••

Bring a saucepan of water to a boil. Score the base of the tomatoes with an x and immerse in the water for 30 seconds. Remove with a slotted spoon and transfer to an ice bath to stop the cooking process. Peel with the tip of a sharp knife, starting at the base end.

ROASTING BELL PEPPERS AND FRESH CHILES

Roasting bell peppers and chiles gives them an attractive smoky and complex flavor. It also makes possible peeling the tough outer skin, which can sometimes be bitter-tasting.

....

Roasting the peppers and chiles can be done on the grill, under the broiler, or on a wire rack placed over a gas flame on top of the stove. Blister and blacken the skins evenly, taking care not to burn the flesh. Transfer to a bowl and cover with plastic wrap; let the peppers and chiles "steam" for about 15 minutes. Uncover, and remove the charred skins with your fingers, or with the tip of a sharp knife. Cut open and remove the seeds and internal ribs—this will help to moderate the heat of the chiles.

Take care to wash your hands thoroughly after handling chiles, and never touch your face or eyes with your hands until you have done so. If you have sensitive skin, wear rubber gloves when handling chiles.

TOASTING SPICES

Toasting spices, such as cumin and coriander seeds, is a technique that brings out more complex flavor tones (it is used especially in Southwestern cuisine). Place the spices in a dry skillet over low heat and toast for about 1 minute, until fragrant, stirring frequently. Take care not to scorch spices or they will taste bitter.

TOASTING SEEDS AND NUTS

This technique intensifies the rich flavor of the seeds or nuts.

For toasted pumpkin seeds, place the seeds in a single layer in a hot, dry skillet over medium-high heat for 2 to 3 minutes, stirring with a wooden spoon. The seeds will pop and brown slightly. Take care not to burn them.

Nuts will take longer to toast. Place on a hot, dry skillet over medium-high heat; pine nuts will take 3 to 5 minutes, and walnuts will take 5 to 7 minutes. You can tell when nuts are toasted—they should brown slightly and become aromatic.

Chestnuts will take longer still because of their size. With a sharp knife, make an x on one side of each nut and place in a dry roasting pan. Cook in a preheated oven at 350 degrees for 35 to 45 minutes, or until soft and tender. Using the tip of a sharp knife, peel back the tough skin by starting with the x incision. Peel off any brown papery skin left on the flesh of the nuts.

CARVING BEEF BRISKET

This method also applies to precooked corned beef brisket.

• •

Carve across the grain of the meat in thin slices, as diagrammed below. We recommend this method because the two muscles of the brisket run in different directions. If the brisket is not sliced properly, it can seem tough or stringy.

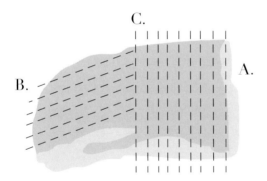

Position the brisket on a slicing board, lean side down. Hold firmly with a fork and begin slicing across the grain of meat at *A*. Continue removing thin slices until you reach the center of the brisket (*C*). Turn the brisket and continue slicing at *B*; you will be slicing across the grain once more.

INDEX